The Clue Books

FLOWERLESS PLANTS

GWEN ALLEN
JOAN DENSLOW

illustrations by
TIM HALLIDAY

OXFORD
UNIVERSITY
PRESS

Oxford University Press, Walton Street, Oxford OX2 6DP

OXFORD NEW YORK TORONTO
DELHI BOMBAY CALCUTTA MADRAS KARACHI
PETALING JAYA SINGAPORE HONG KONG TOKYO
NAIROBI DAR ES SALAAM CAPE TOWN
MELBOURNE AUCKLAND

and associated companies in
BERLIN IBADAN

Oxford is a trade mark of Oxford University Press

FIRST PUBLISHED 1973
REPRINTED 1975, 1981, 1983, 1986, 1991

FILMSET BT BAS PRINTERS LIMITED, WALLOP, HAMPSHIRE
PRINTED IN HONG KONG

FERNS
pages 52—57

MOSSES
pages 44—49

HORSETAILS
pages 60,61

LIVERWORTS
page 42

This book is about flowerless plants.
These plants do not produce flowers or seeds, but grow from *spores* which are produced in *fruiting bodies.*

If your plant looks like one of these, turn to the pages shown.
In order to name your plant you will need to use the clues.

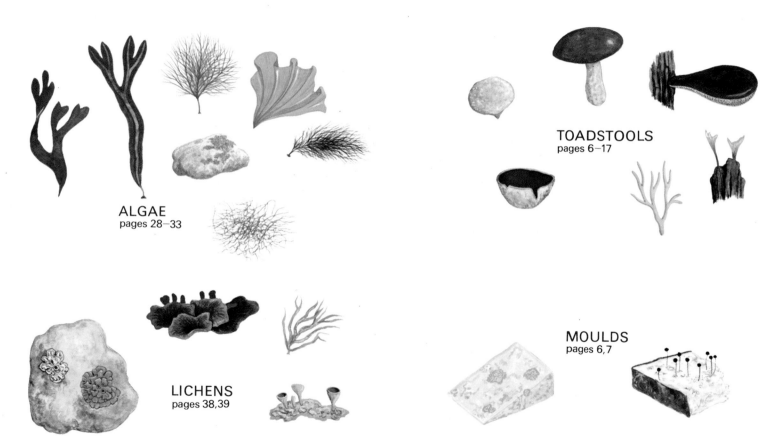

ALGAE
pages 28–33

TOADSTOOLS
pages 6–17

LICHENS
pages 38,39

MOULDS
pages 6,7

Most of the coloured illustrations are drawn the same size as the real plant. But when the plant is too big to be drawn life-size, the true measurement is given beside the drawing, e.g. 30 cm.

Make a collection of flowerless plants, except FERNS (see pages 2 and 3) from waste ground, walls, banks, woods, downland, sandy heaths, or from your garden or park. Always ask the park keeper before taking anything from a park.

You will need polythene bags, plastic boxes or tins with lids to put your specimens in, a penknife to help you to remove small plants carefully, a magnifying lens to help you see the plants more clearly, and white adhesive tape to make labels.

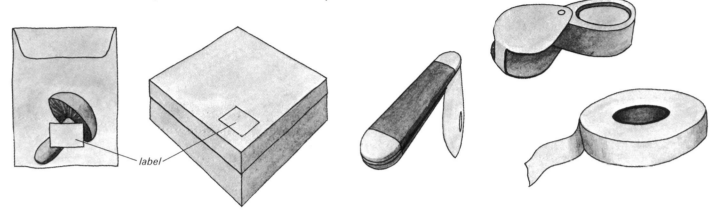

label

When you are naming the plants you have collected, it is often helpful to know exactly where you found them growing. The best way to record this is to have several labelled polythene bags. As you collect the plants, put them into the correct bag.

on a wall

on soil

on trunk of Beech

Collect pieces big enough to see exactly what the whole plant looks like, but be careful not to damage the other plants around it.
Unless there are several like it, do not take the whole plant.

HOW TO KEEP, MOUNT, AND NAME FLOWERLESS PLANTS

Most flowerless plants, except toadstools, seaweeds, and horsetails, may be kept for several weeks in enclosed containers. If you keep them in a light place the green plants will make sugar and oxygen from water and the carbon-dioxide which they breathe out. In this way they will have a continual supply of food, fresh air, and moisture.

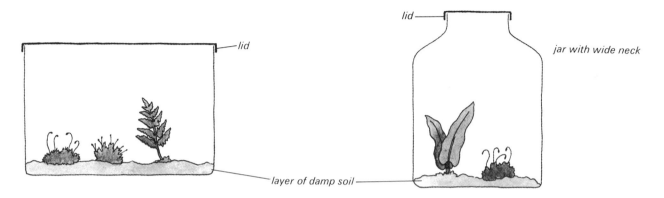

Mount small pieces of each plant on card under clear self-adhesive plastic, and keep them in a book. Write the name, the date on which you found it, and where it was growing, beside each one.

In order to use the clues for naming your plants, first turn to pages 2 and 3; find the clue that fits it, and turn to the page given for the next clue. Repeat this until you find its group or name.

Only the most common plants in each group have been illustrated in this book: if, when you have found the group to which your plant belongs, the particular plant is not shown, look up the group in another book that gives details of more flowerless plants (see page 64).

MOULDS AND TOADSTOOLS

Moulds and toadstools belong to the group called FUNGI. The fungus plant is a
mass of white threads called *hyphae* which grow and feed on dead plant and animal remains.
The plants produce *fruiting bodies*, which are the parts we most often see and call moulds
and toadstools.

Look for hyphae among rotten leaves
and dead wood.
Put some on a glass slide and look
at them under a microscope.

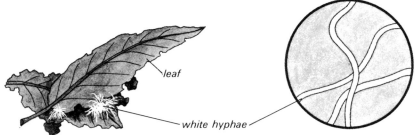

leaf

white hyphae

MOULDS

Moulds are very small fungi. Their spores (see page 3) float in air or water. Some of them swim.

Collect as many moulds as you can from cheese, bread, fruit, and other things, or grow some.

fruiting bodies

hyphae in bread

fruit

blue or white
powdery fruiting
bodies

cheese

HOW TO GROW MOULDS

You will need a piece of bread and a clean plastic dish
with a lid.
Put the bread in the dish, pour on enough water to make
it wet, and leave it in the room for half an hour to
allow the spores from the air to fall on it. Put the lid
on and leave it in a warm place.
You should be able to see the fruiting bodies after a few days.

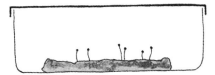

In order to see the moulds more clearly, use a needle or tweezers to separate a small quantity of the mould, put it on a glass slide, and examine it under a microscope.

Look for fruiting bodies. They may look like these.

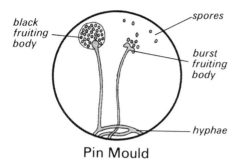

Pin Mould

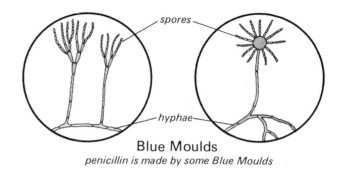

Blue Moulds
penicillin is made by some Blue Moulds

HOW TO GROW WATER MOULDS

You will need ants' 'eggs' (bought from a pet shop). Float these in a dish of pond or river water and leave them in a warm place. After a few days you should be able to see the hyphae.

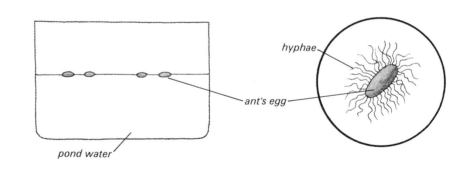

In order to see your moulds more clearly, use a needle or tweezers to separate a small quantity of mould, put it in a drop of water on a glass slide and examine it under a microscope.

Look for the fruiting bodies. They may look like these.

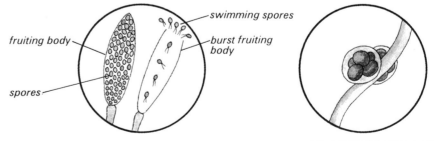

another kind of fruiting body

8

TOADSTOOLS

Make a collection of as many different kinds of toadstools (fruiting bodies) as possible from woods and fields.

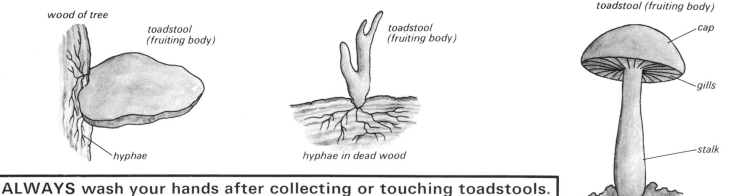

ALWAYS wash your hands after collecting or touching toadstools.

DO NOT eat them unless you are quite sure they are edible.

To keep records of your toadstools
you can: take photographs
draw or paint them
make spore prints (see opposite)

and although it is not possible to preserve whole toadstools you can cut a thin slice down the middle and mount it under clear self-adhesive plastic.

You can keep your collection in a Toadstool Book.

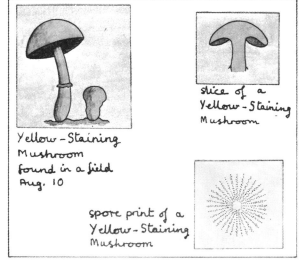

A page from a Toadstool Book

When the spores (see p. 3) produced in the toadstools are ripe, they float in the air, and, when they land on food, grow into new hyphae.

You can see spores if you put a thin gill from an *Agaric* (see page 10, clue 1) or a scraping from the inside of a Cup Toadstool (see page 11, clue 5) on a glass slide and look at it under a microscope.

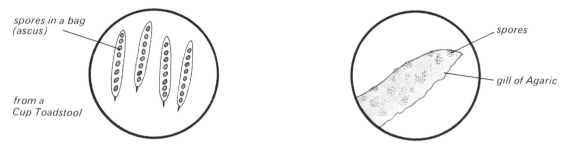

spores in a bag (ascus)

from a Cup Toadstool

spores

gill of Agaric

HOW TO MAKE A SPORE PRINT

Find a fully grown Agaric Toadstool which is still fresh. Cut off the stem and put the cap, gills downwards, on a piece of plastic. Cover it with a box or jar to keep it free from draughts, and leave it overnight.

Next morning carefully remove the box and cap: the spores will have fallen from the gills and made a print on the plastic. Cover the print with clear self-adhesive plastic.

In order to see the colour of the spores more clearly mount the plastic on either white or coloured paper. Add it to your Toadstool Book.

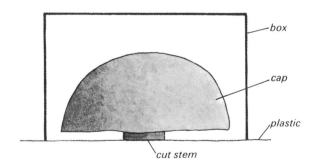

box

cap

plastic

cut stem

CLUES TO NAMING TOADSTOOLS

1. If the fruiting body has a cap with gills underneath, on which the spores (see page 3) grow, it is a GILLED MUSHROOM or TOADSTOOL (Agaric);

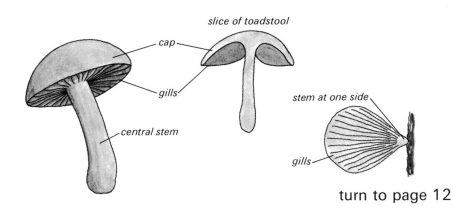

turn to page 12

2. If the fruiting body has a thick, spongy cap with tubes underneath, in which the spores grow, it is a SPONGE TOADSTOOL (Boletus);

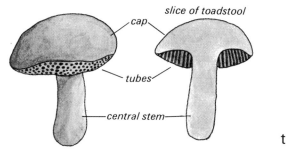

turn to page 25

3. If the fruiting body grows on trees, has tubes underneath in which the spores grow, and most often looks like a bracket or a shelf, it is a BRACKET TOADSTOOL (Polypore);

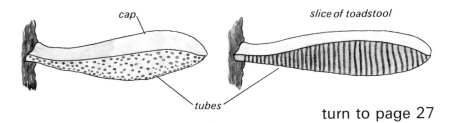

turn to page 27

4. If the fruiting body grows on wood, looks like a thin crust or bracket or shelf, but does not have tubes underneath, it is a SKIN TOADSTOOL (Thelophore);

turn to page 27

continued from page 10

5. If the fruiting body is more
    or less cup-shaped, with
    smooth or frilly edges, it
    may be a CUP TOADSTOOL (Peziza),
    HORN OF PLENTY (Craterellus),
    or JELLY TOADSTOOL;

turn to pages 21, 26

6. If the fruiting body looks
    like this and smells strongly
    of rotten meat, it is a
    STINKHORN;

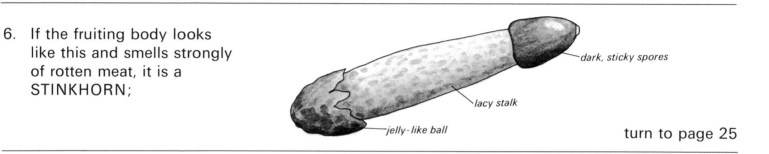

dark, sticky spores

lacy stalk

jelly-like ball

turn to page 25

7. If the fruiting body is a
    roundish ball;

turn to page 25

8. If the fruiting body is
    slender, leathery, has one
    or more branches that
    may be flattened or
    clublike at the ends;

turn to page 26

From page 10, clue 1

In order to name your gilled Toadstools you need to know the colour of their spores, because they are grouped according to their spore colour. The gills are most often the same colour as the spores, but you should check this by making a spore print (see page 9).

CLUES TO NAMING AGARICS

1. If the spores are white, cream, pale yellow, pale pink or pale violet, see clues 1 and 2 at the foot of this page and clue 3 on page 13

---

2. If the spores are deep pink

turn to top of page 17, clues 1—3

---

3. If the spores are rusty-brown

turn to page 16

---

4. If the spores are purple or black

turn to bottom of page 17, clues 1—3

From clue 1 above

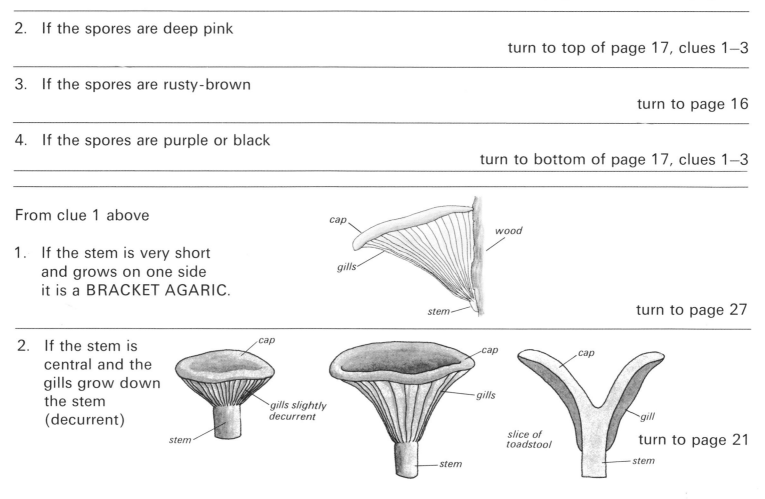

1. If the stem is very short and grows on one side it is a BRACKET AGARIC.

turn to page 27

---

2. If the stem is central and the gills grow down the stem (decurrent)

turn to page 21

cap

gill

slices of toadstools

gills not joined to stem

stem

stem

gills joined to stem

continued from page 12

3. If the stem is central and the gills are not decurrent

see below and page 14, clue 4

From clue 3 above

1. If the toadstool has both a ring and a volva (frilly base), it is an AMANITA (poisonous).

cap

gills

fleshy ring

frilly base (volva)

turn to page 18

2. If the toadstool has a ring but no volva it may be a PARASOL MUSHROOM (Lepiota) or a HONEY TOADSTOOL (Armillaria).

cap

gills

fleshy ring

turn to page 19

3. If the toadstool has a volva but no ring it is a GRISETTE.

cap 4 – 9 cm orange-brown or grey

(not illustrated elsewhere in this book)

frilly volva

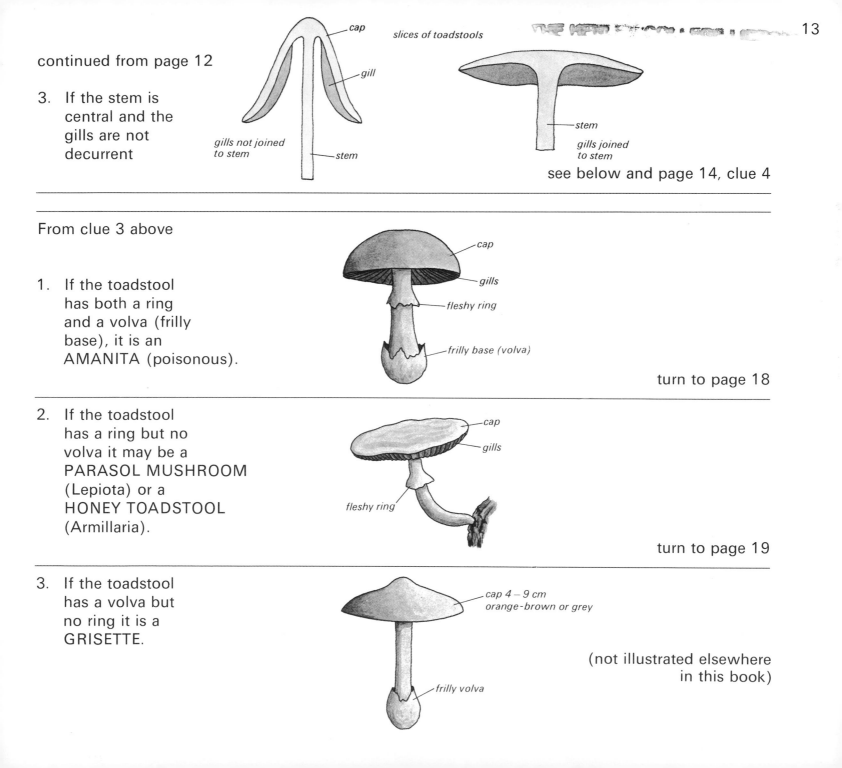

continued from page 13

4. If the toadstool
    has neither a ring
    nor a volva

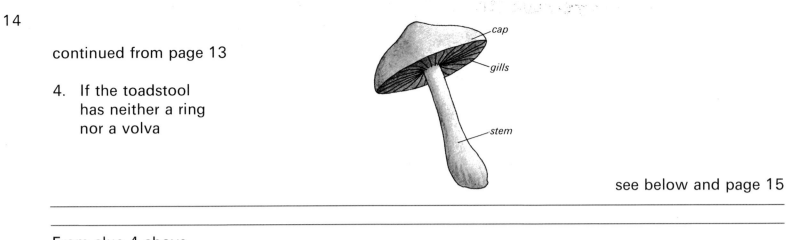

see below and page 15

From clue 4 above

1. If the toadstool has a cap, stem, and gills of the same yellowish-red or violet colour,
    it may be LACCARIA.

turn to page 18

2. If the toadstool
    has thick, waxy
    gills and often a
    slimy cap, it may
    be a WAX CAP
    (Hygrophorus).

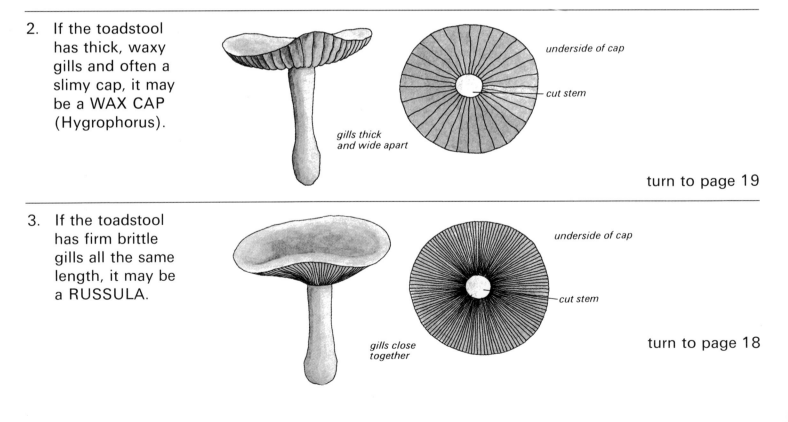

underside of cap

cut stem

gills thick
and wide apart

turn to page 19

3. If the toadstool
    has firm brittle
    gills all the same
    length, it may be
    a RUSSULA.

underside of cap

cut stem

gills close
together

turn to page 18

continued from page 14

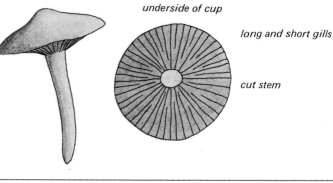

underside of cup

long and short gills

cut stem

4. If the toadstool has gills
    of different lengths, a
    tough, firm (not stringy)
    stem greater than 5 mm
    in diameter, it may be a
    TRICHOLOMA.

turn to page 19

5. If the toadstool has a
    tough stringy (fibrous)
    stem, and the edge of the
    cap rolls inwards, it
    may be a
    SHANK TOADSTOOL
    (Collybia).

cap

rolled edge

stringy stem

turn to page 20

6. If the toadstool has a
    thin stem (less than 5 mm
    in diameter) a soft, thin
    conical cap through
    which the gills may be
    seen, and is not rolled
    inwards at the edge, it may
    be a STRIPED BONNET
    (Mycena).

striped cap

slender stem

turn to page 20

7. If the toadstool is tough
    and leathery when dry, and
    the cap, which becomes more
    or less flat, often rolls
    inward at the edge, it may
    be a MARASMIUS.

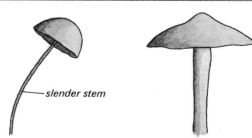

slender stem

turn to page 20

From page 12, clue 3

1. If the stem is short and grows to one side of the cap, it may be a BRACKET AGARIC (Crepidotus).

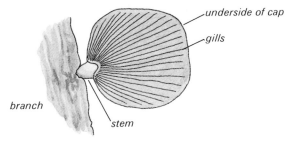

turn to page 27

2. If the stem is in the middle or a little to one side and the gills grow down the stem (decurrent), it may be PAXILLUS.

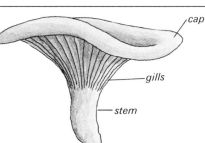

turn to page 22

3. If the gills are not decurrent, and there is a ring on the stem, it may be PHOLIOTA.

turn to page 22

4. If the toadstool has neither a ring nor decurrent gills, but has a cobweb-like veil beneath the cap when young, it may be a VEIL TOADSTOOL (Cortinarius).

turn to page 22

5. If the toadstool does not look like these

turn to page 22

From top of page 12, clue 2

1. If the gills grow down the
   stem (decurrent) and the
   cap becomes cup-shaped
   with frilly edges, it is
   THE MILLER (Clitopilus).

turn to page 23

2. If the cap is thin, most
   often striped, and shaped
   like a Chinese hat, it is a
   CHINESE HAT TOADSTOOL
   (Rhodophyllus).

turn to page 23

3. If the toadstool does not look like these it may be FAWN PLUTEUS or LEADEN ENTOLOMA.

turn to page 23

From page 12, clue 4

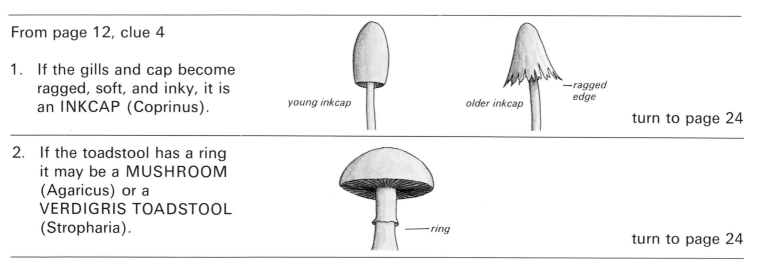

1. If the gills and cap become
   ragged, soft, and inky, it is
   an INKCAP (Coprinus).

young inkcap

older inkcap

—ragged edge

turn to page 24

2. If the toadstool has a ring
   it may be a MUSHROOM
   (Agaricus) or a
   VERDIGRIS TOADSTOOL
   (Stropharia).

—ring

turn to page 24

3. If the toadstool does not look like any of these

turn to pages 23, 24

AGARICS WITH WHITE SPORES

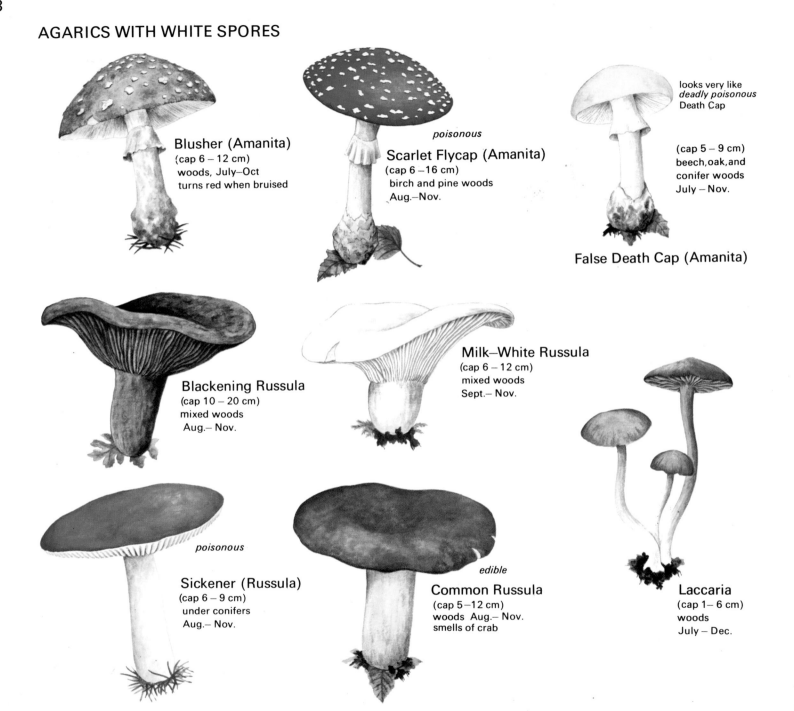

Blusher (Amanita)
(cap 6 – 12 cm)
woods, July–Oct
turns red when bruised

poisonous
Scarlet Flycap (Amanita)
(cap 6 –16 cm)
birch and pine woods
Aug.–Nov.

looks very like
deadly poisonous
Death Cap

(cap 5 – 9 cm)
beech, oak, and
conifer woods
July – Nov.

False Death Cap (Amanita)

Blackening Russula
(cap 10 – 20 cm)
mixed woods
Aug.– Nov.

Milk–White Russula
(cap 6 – 12 cm)
mixed woods
Sept.– Nov.

poisonous
Sickener (Russula)
(cap 6 – 9 cm)
under conifers
Aug.– Nov.

edible
Common Russula
(cap 5–12 cm)
woods Aug.– Nov.
smells of crab

Laccaria
(cap 1– 6 cm)
woods
July – Dec.

AGARICS WITH WHITE SPORES

edible

**Wood Blewits
(Tricholoma)**
(cap 6 – 10 cm)
woods, gardens
Oct.– Dec.

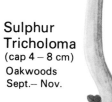

**Sulphur
Tricholoma**
(cap 4 – 8 cm)
Oakwoods
Sept.– Nov.

**Soap–Scented
Tricholoma**
(cap 3 – 8 cm)
woods, Aug. – Nov.

edible

**Parasol Mushroom
(Lepiota)**
(cap 10 – 20 cm)
grassy places
July – Nov. ·

edible

moveable ring

**Honey Toadstool
(Armillaria)**
(cap 3 – 10 cm)
on trees
July – Dec.

Scarlet Wax Cap
(cap 2 – 5 cm)
in grass near woods
July – Dec.

edible

**Buff Wax Cap
(Hygrophorus)**
(cap 2 – 7 cm)
grasslands
Aug.– Dec.

edible

**Parrot
Wax Cap**
(cap 1 – 3 cm)
short grass,
copses
July – Nov.

AGARICS WITH WHITE SPORES

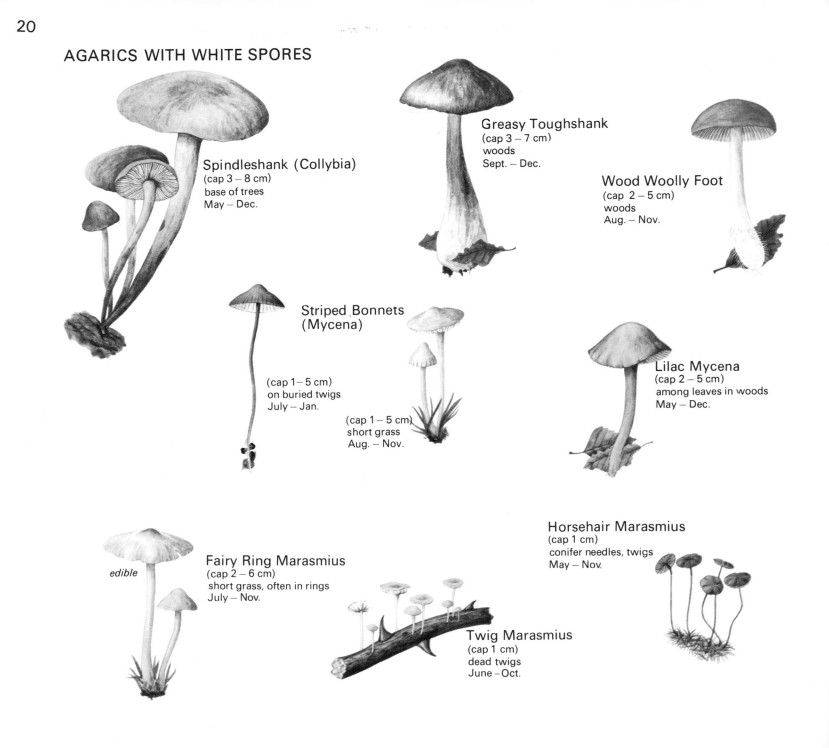

Spindleshank (Collybia)
(cap 3 – 8 cm)
base of trees
May – Dec.

Greasy Toughshank
(cap 3 – 7 cm)
woods
Sept. – Dec.

Wood Woolly Foot
(cap 2 – 5 cm)
woods
Aug. – Nov.

**Striped Bonnets
(Mycena)**

(cap 1 – 5 cm)
on buried twigs
July – Jan.

(cap 1 – 5 cm)
short grass
Aug. – Nov.

Lilac Mycena
(cap 2 – 5 cm)
among leaves in woods
May – Dec.

Horsehair Marasmius
(cap 1 cm)
conifer needles, twigs
May – Nov.

edible

Fairy Ring Marasmius
(cap 2 – 6 cm)
short grass, often in rings
July – Nov.

Twig Marasmius
(cap 1 cm)
dead twigs
June – Oct.

AGARICS WITH WHITE SPORES

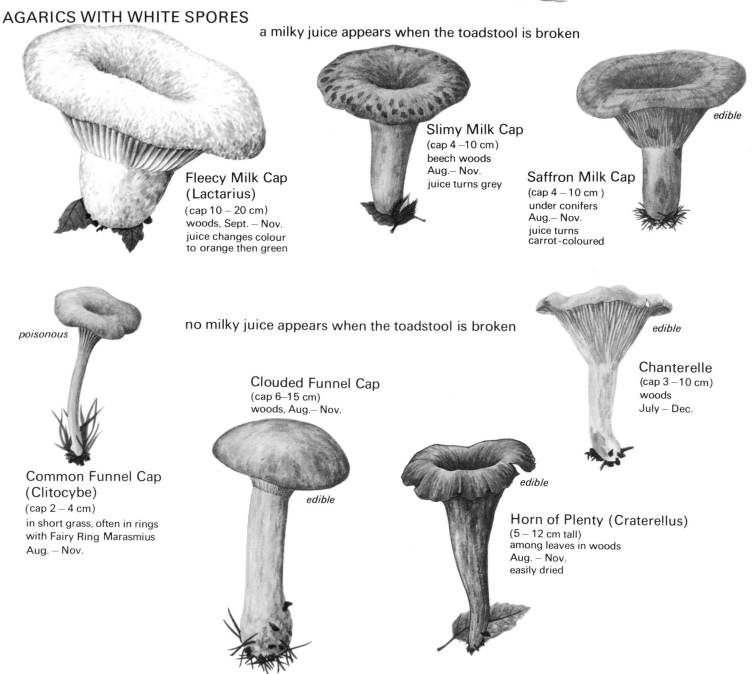

a milky juice appears when the toadstool is broken

**Fleecy Milk Cap
(Lactarius)**
(cap 10 – 20 cm)
woods, Sept. – Nov.
juice changes colour
to orange then green

Slimy Milk Cap
(cap 4 –10 cm)
beech woods
Aug.– Nov.
juice turns grey

Saffron Milk Cap
(cap 4 – 10 cm)
under conifers
Aug.– Nov.
juice turns
carrot-coloured

edible

no milky juice appears when the toadstool is broken

poisonous

**Common Funnel Cap
(Clitocybe)**
(cap 2 – 4 cm)
in short grass, often in rings
with Fairy Ring Marasmius
Aug. – Nov.

Clouded Funnel Cap
(cap 6–15 cm)
woods, Aug.– Nov.

edible

edible

Horn of Plenty (Craterellus)
(5 – 12 cm tall)
among leaves in woods
Aug. – Nov.
easily dried

edible

Chanterelle
(cap 3 –10 cm)
woods
July – Dec.

AGARICS WITH RUSTY BROWN SPORES

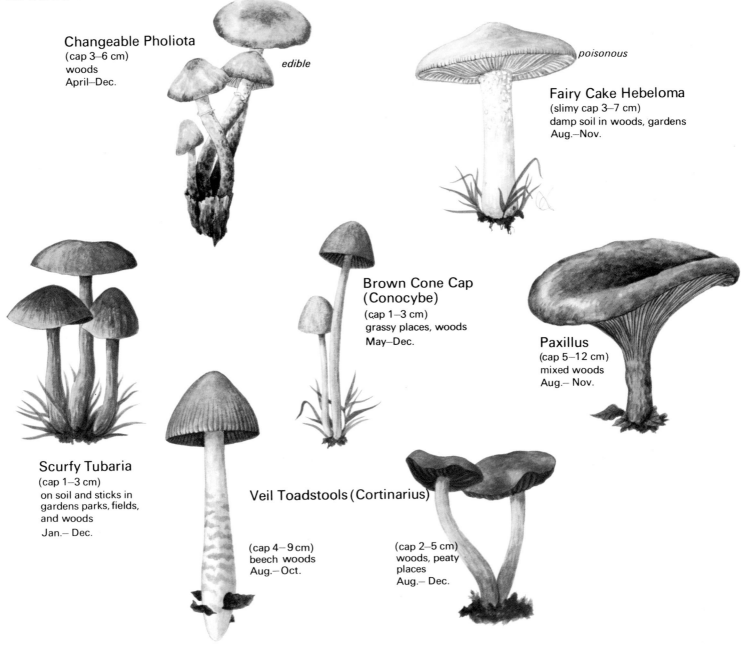

Changeable Pholiota
(cap 3–6 cm)
woods
April–Dec.

edible

poisonous

Fairy Cake Hebeloma
(slimy cap 3–7 cm)
damp soil in woods, gardens
Aug.–Nov.

**Brown Cone Cap
(Conocybe)**
(cap 1–3 cm)
grassy places, woods
May–Dec.

Paxillus
(cap 5–12 cm)
mixed woods
Aug.– Nov.

Scurfy Tubaria
(cap 1–3 cm)
on soil and sticks in
gardens parks, fields,
and woods
Jan.– Dec.

Veil Toadstools (Cortinarius)

(cap 4–9 cm)
beech woods
Aug.–Oct.

(cap 2–5 cm)
woods, peaty
places
Aug.– Dec.

AGARICS WITH DEEP PINK SPORES

**Chinese Hat Toadstool
(Rhodophyllus)**
(cap 2–6 cm)
short grass
May.– Oct.

poisonous

Leaden Entoloma
(cap 7–12 cm)
woods
Aug.–Nov.
may be mistaken for
mushrooms

Fawn Pluteus
(cap 3–8 cm)
rotten wood,
old stumps
Jan.– Dec.

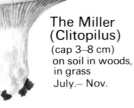

**The Miller
(Clitopilus)**
(cap 3–8 cm)
on soil in woods,
in grass
July.– Nov.

AGARICS WITH PURPLE-BLACK SPORES

**Graceful Brittle Cap
(Psathyrella)**
(cap 1–3 cm)
among leaves and sticks
Aug.– Nov.

Common Brittle Cap
(cap 2–6 cm)
densely tufted on or near
tree stumps
Aug.– Nov.

**Crumble Cap
(Coprinus)**
(cap 0·5 cm tall)
clustered round
old stumps
May – Nov.

AGARICS WITH BLACK OR PURPLE-BLACK SPORES

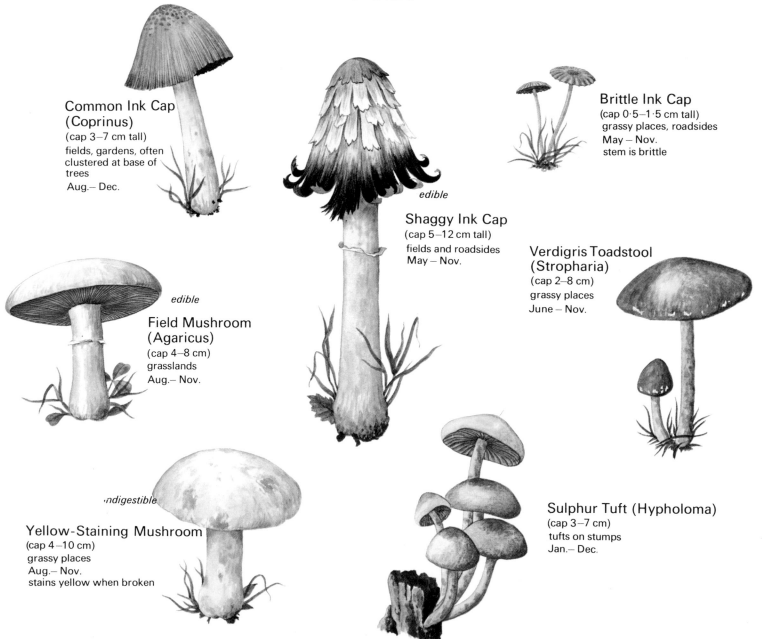

**Common Ink Cap
(Coprinus)**
(cap 3–7 cm tall)
fields, gardens, often
clustered at base of
trees
Aug.– Dec.

edible

Shaggy Ink Cap
(cap 5–12 cm tall)
fields and roadsides
May – Nov.

Brittle Ink Cap
(cap 0·5–1·5 cm tall)
grassy places, roadsides
May – Nov.
stem is brittle

edible

**Field Mushroom
(Agaricus)**
(cap 4–8 cm)
grasslands
Aug.– Nov.

**Verdigris Toadstool
(Stropharia)**
(cap 2–8 cm)
grassy places
June – Nov.

indigestible

Yellow-Staining Mushroom
(cap 4–10 cm)
grassy places
Aug.– Nov.
stains yellow when broken

Sulphur Tuft (Hypholoma)
(cap 3–7 cm)
tufts on stumps
Jan.– Dec.

SPONGE TOADSTOOLS (Boletus)

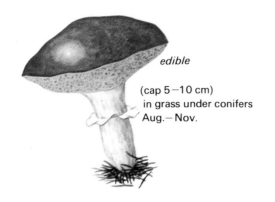

edible

(cap 5–10 cm)
in grass under conifers
Aug.–Nov.

edible

(cap 5–12 cm)
under larch,
Mar.–Nov.
flesh turns violet
when broken

(cap 4–10 cm)
woods, Aug.–Nov.
when broken flesh
changes colour to blue,
then red, then buff

BALL-LIKE TOADSTOOLS

Puffball (Lycoperdon)
(4–7 cm tall)
on grass in woods
July–Nov.

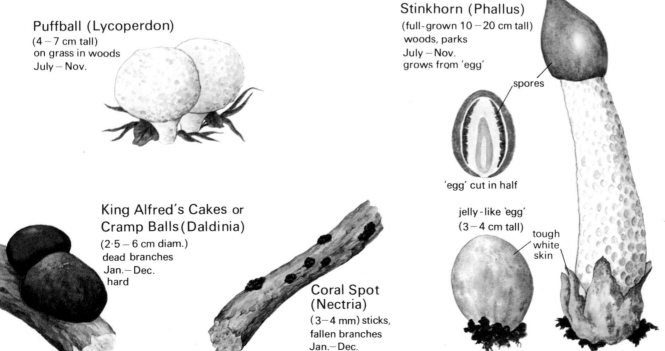

King Alfred's Cakes or Cramp Balls (Daldinia)
(2·5–6 cm diam.)
dead branches
Jan.–Dec.
hard

Coral Spot (Nectria)
(3–4 mm) sticks,
fallen branches
Jan.–Dec.

Stinkhorn (Phallus)
(full-grown 10–20 cm tall)
woods, parks
July–Nov.
grows from 'egg'

spores

'egg' cut in half

jelly-like 'egg'
(3–4 cm tall)

tough
white
skin

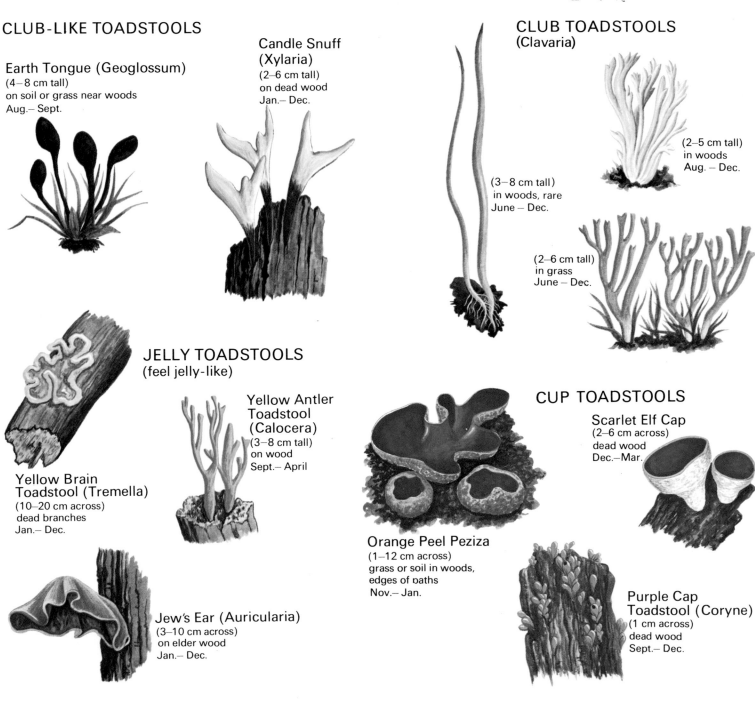

CLUB-LIKE TOADSTOOLS

Earth Tongue (Geoglossum)
(4–8 cm tall)
on soil or grass near woods
Aug.– Sept.

**Candle Snuff
(Xylaria)**
(2–6 cm tall)
on dead wood
Jan.– Dec.

CLUB TOADSTOOLS
(Clavaria)

(2–5 cm tall)
in woods
Aug. – Dec.

(3–8 cm tall)
in woods, rare
June – Dec.

(2–6 cm tall)
in grass
June – Dec.

JELLY TOADSTOOLS
(feel jelly-like)

**Yellow Antler
Toadstool
(Calocera)**
(3–8 cm tall)
on wood
Sept.– April

**Yellow Brain
Toadstool (Tremella)**
(10–20 cm across)
dead branches
Jan.– Dec.

Jew's Ear (Auricularia)
(3–10 cm across)
on elder wood
Jan.– Dec.

CUP TOADSTOOLS

Scarlet Elf Cap
(2–6 cm across)
dead wood
Dec.–Mar.

Orange Peel Peziza
(1–12 cm across)
grass or soil in woods,
edges of paths
Nov.– Jan.

**Purple Cap
Toadstool (Coryne)**
(1 cm across)
dead wood
Sept.– Dec.

BRACKET TOADSTOOLS (POLYPORES)

Shaggy Polypore
(10—30 cm across)
elm and ash trunks
April — Oct.

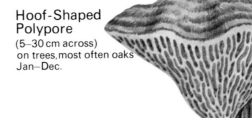

Hoof-Shaped Polypore
(5—30 cm across)
on trees, most often oaks
Jan—Dec.

Birch Polypore
(5—30 cm across)
birch trees
Jan.— Dec.

Polystictus
(3—5 cm across)
stumps and branches
Jan.— Dec.

SKIN TOADSTOOLS (THELOPHORES)
on dead branches

Hairy Stereum
(1—4 cm across)

Stereum
(1—3 cm across)

Corticum
(1—4 cm across)

BRACKET AGARICS

Panellus
(1—3 cm)
on stumps
Jan.— Dec.
spores white

Soft Slipper Toadstool (Crepidotus)
(1—5 cm)
on wood
July — Nov.
spores rusty brown

edible

Oyster Mushroom (Pleurotus)
(3—17 cm)
on trees
Jan.— Dec.
spores pale lilac

ALGAE

Algae are green plants that have neither leaves nor roots. They grow on old fences, tree trunks, wet soil, in fresh and sea water.

Collect as many different algae as you can: if they are small, mount some in a drop of water on a glass slide and look at it under a microscope.

CLUES TO NAMING ALGAE

1. If the plant is green, and grows on fences, trees, wet soil, or in fresh water

go to 1 and 2 below

---

2. If the plant is red, brown or green and grows in the sea or on the seashore it is a SEAWEED.

turn to page 30

From clue 1 above

1. If the plant is green and powdery
    it may be a POWDERY ALGA.
    (See also Lichens, pages 38, 39.)

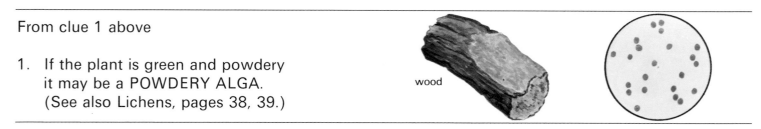

wood

2. If the plant is made up of green threads called filaments, it is a FILAMENTOUS ALGA, often called BLANKET WEED.

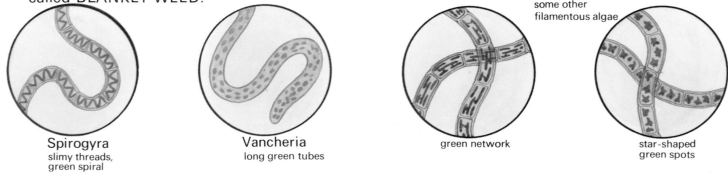

some other filamentous algae

Spirogyra
slimy threads,
green spiral

Vancheria
long green tubes

green network

star-shaped
green spots

If you wish to know more about green algae you will need to look in other books (see page 64).

SEAWEEDS

Seaweeds cling with a holdfast to rocks and other weeds on the seashore.

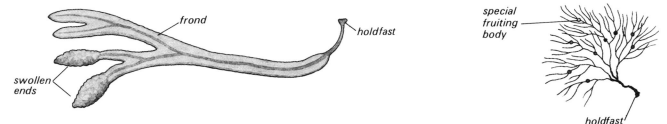

The leaflike parts of the plants are called *fronds*. The brown and red pigments of seaweeds help to trap light that reaches them through the water (see page 5).
If you put some seaweed in a dish and pour boiling water on it, the red or brown pigment will ooze out, leaving the green pigment in the frond.

Spores (see page 3) may grow in swollen ends of fronds or in special fruiting bodies which burst when ripe. The spores escape into the sea, settle on rocks or other seaweeds, and grow into new plants.

HOW TO MOUNT SEAWEEDS

Press large seaweeds and cover them with clear self-adhesive plastic.

In order to mount small seaweeds you will need to float out small pieces in a saucepan of seawater. (The colour may fade if you use tap water.)

Slip a piece of paper underneath the weed and lift it carefully out of the water, keeping the weed spread out over the paper.

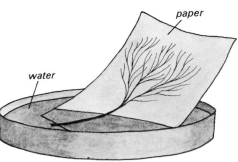

When the paper and weed have dried, cover with clear self-adhesive plastic. Add it to your collection. Label it (see page 5).

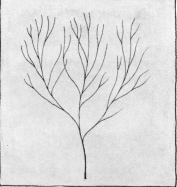

From page 28, clue 2

1. If it is a green seaweed

go to clues 1–3 below and page 31, clue 4

2. If it is a brown seaweed

turn to pages 31–32

3. If it is a red seaweed

turn to page 33

From clue 1 above

1. If the seaweed frond
    is like a large, thin
    leaf, it may be
    SEA LETTUCE (Ulva).

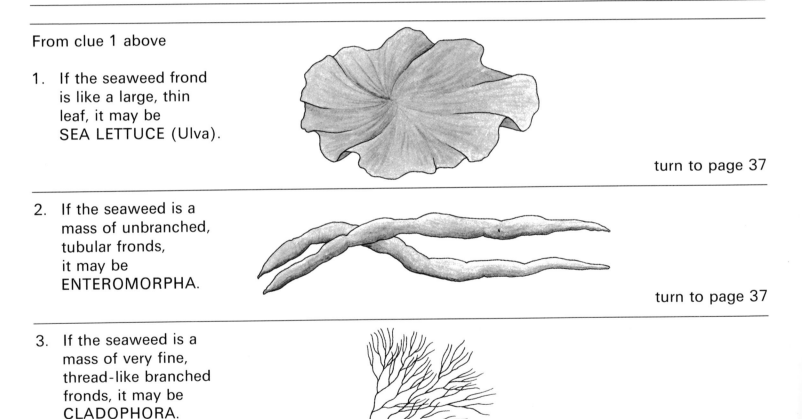

turn to page 37

2. If the seaweed is a
    mass of unbranched,
    tubular fronds,
    it may be
    ENTEROMORPHA.

turn to page 37

3. If the seaweed is a
    mass of very fine,
    thread-like branched
    fronds, it may be
    CLADOPHORA.

turn to page 37

Continued from page 30, green seaweeds

4. If the seaweed is thick
    and branched, and feels
    velvety and spongy, it
    is CODIUM.

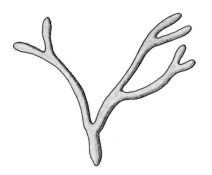

turn to page 37

From top of page 30, clue 2, brown seaweeds

1. If the frond is very large,
    single, sometimes divided
    at the end, and has a
    branched holdfast, it is
    an OARWEED (Laminaria).

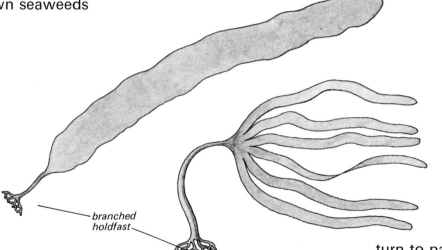

branched
holdfast

turn to page 34

2. If the frond is large, branched,
    (always dividing into two
    at each branch) and has a
    flattened holdfast, it may
    be a WRACK (Fucus).

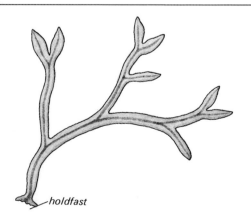

holdfast

turn to page 35

continued from page 31

3. If the fronds are slender,
    stiff, and branched, it may
    be SHRUBBY SEAWEED
    (Cystoseira).

turn to page 34

---

4. If the fronds are very fine,
    thread-like, and grow on
    rocks or other seaweeds, it
    is either ECTOCARPUS or a
    TUFTED BROWN SEAWEED.

turn to pages 34, 35

---

5. If the fronds look like one of these, turn to the page shown.

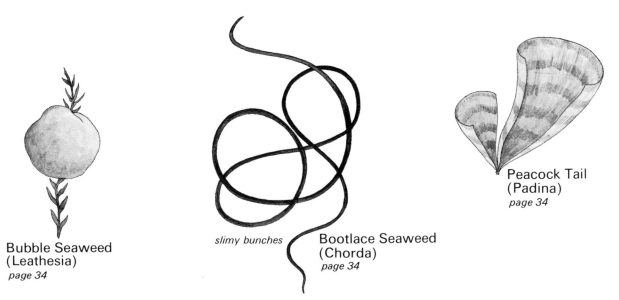

Bubble Seaweed
(Leathesia)
page 34

slimy bunches   Bootlace Seaweed
(Chorda)
page 34

Peacock Tail
(Padina)
page 34

From top of page 30, clue 3

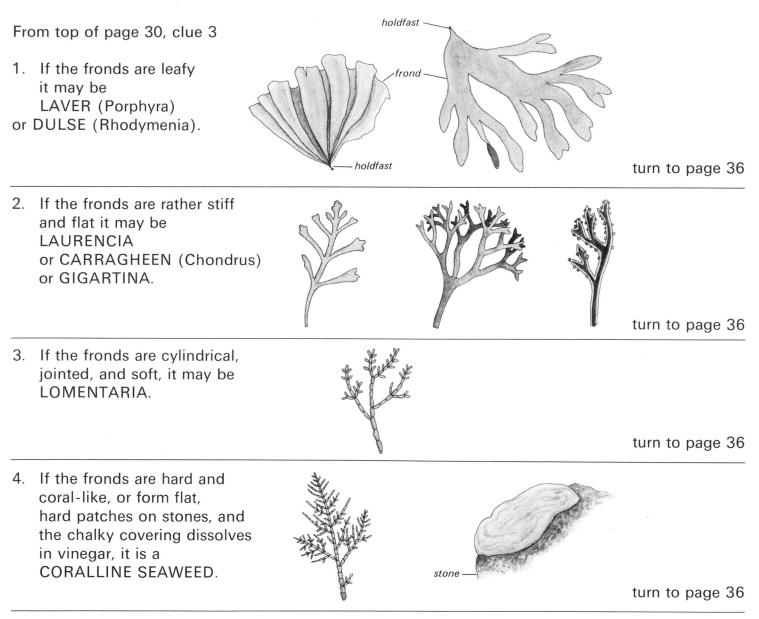

1. If the fronds are leafy
   it may be
   LAVER (Porphyra)
   or DULSE (Rhodymenia).

turn to page 36

2. If the fronds are rather stiff
   and flat it may be
   LAURENCIA
   or CARRAGHEEN (Chondrus)
   or GIGARTINA.

turn to page 36

3. If the fronds are cylindrical,
   jointed, and soft, it may be
   LOMENTARIA.

turn to page 36

4. If the fronds are hard and
   coral-like, or form flat,
   hard patches on stones, and
   the chalky covering dissolves
   in vinegar, it is a
   CORALLINE SEAWEED.

turn to page 36

5. If the fronds are divided into numerous slender branches

turn to page 37

BROWN ALGAE from page 32

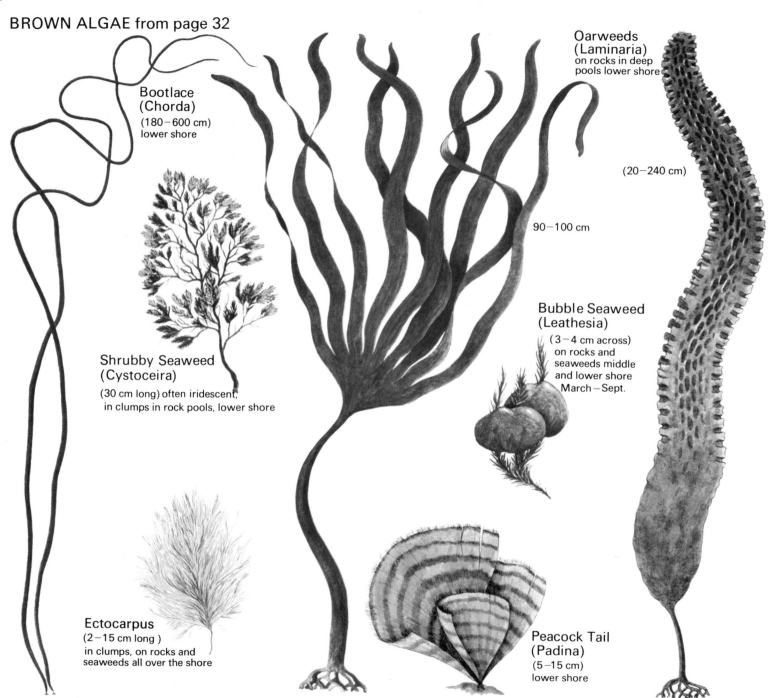

**Bootlace
(Chorda)**
(180−600 cm)
lower shore

**Oarweeds
(Laminaria)**
on rocks in deep
pools lower shore

(20−240 cm)

90−100 cm

**Shrubby Seaweed
(Cystoceira)**
(30 cm long) often iridescent,
in clumps in rock pools, lower shore

**Bubble Seaweed
(Leathesia)**
(3−4 cm across)
on rocks and
seaweeds middle
and lower shore
March−Sept.

Ectocarpus
(2−15 cm long)
in clumps, on rocks and
seaweeds all over the shore

**Peacock Tail
(Padina)**
(5−15 cm)
lower shore

BROWN SEAWEEDS WRACKS (FUCUS) on all rocky shores

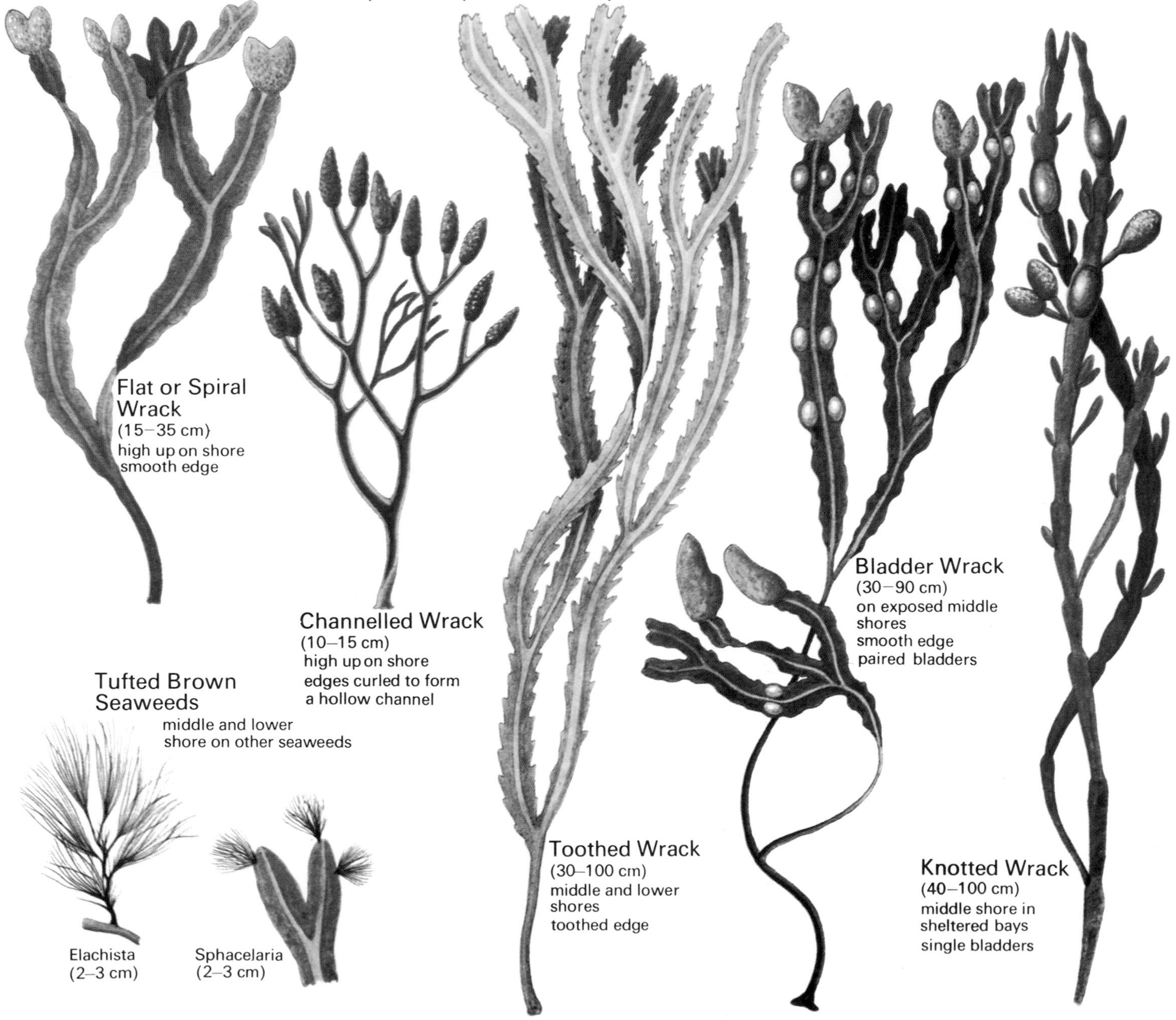

Flat or Spiral Wrack
(15—35 cm)
high up on shore
smooth edge

Channelled Wrack
(10—15 cm)
high up on shore
edges curled to form
a hollow channel

Tufted Brown Seaweeds
middle and lower
shore on other seaweeds

Elachista
(2—3 cm)

Sphacelaria
(2—3 cm)

Toothed Wrack
(30—100 cm)
middle and lower
shores
toothed edge

Bladder Wrack
(30—90 cm)
on exposed middle
shores
smooth edge
paired bladders

Knotted Wrack
(40—100 cm)
middle shore in
sheltered bays
single bladders

RED SEAWEEDS middle and lower shore in rock pools

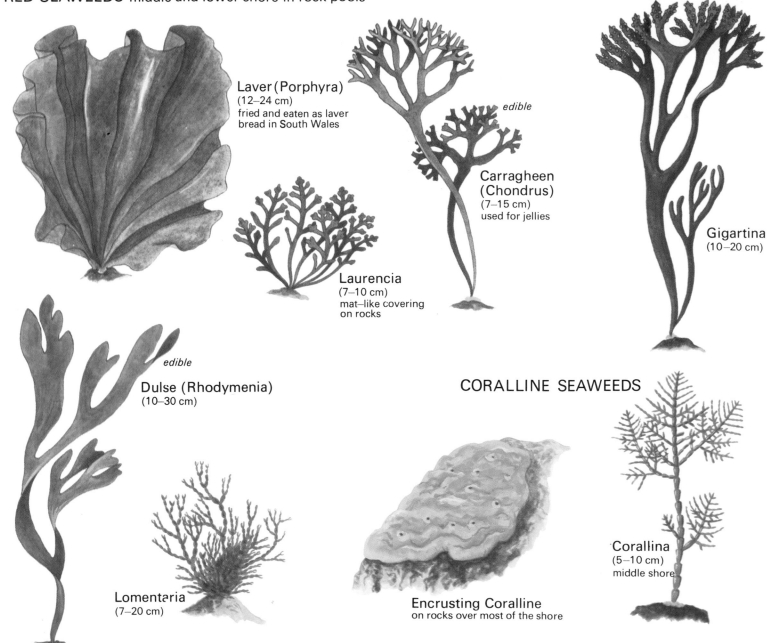

Laver (Porphyra)
(12–24 cm)
fried and eaten as laver
bread in South Wales

edible

Carragheen
(Chondrus)
(7–15 cm)
used for jellies

Laurencia
(7–10 cm)
mat–like covering
on rocks

Gigartina
(10–20 cm)

edible

Dulse (Rhodymenia)
(10–30 cm)

CORALLINE SEAWEEDS

Lomentaria
(7–20 cm)

Encrusting Coralline
on rocks over most of the shore

Corallina
(5–10 cm)
middle shore

RED SEAWEEDS middle and lower shores in rock pools

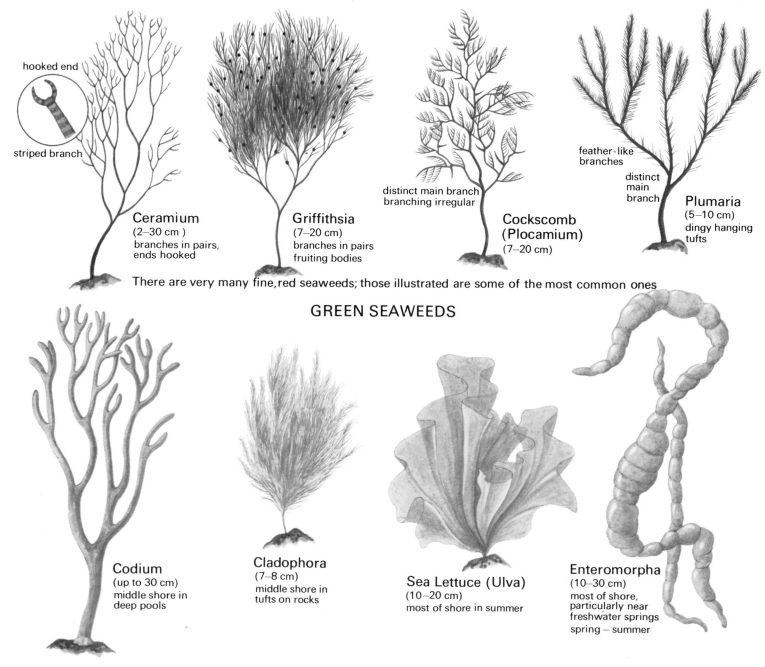

hooked end

striped branch

Ceramium
(2–30 cm)
branches in pairs,
ends hooked

Griffithsia
(7–20 cm)
branches in pairs
fruiting bodies

distinct main branch
branching irregular

**Cockscomb
(Plocamium)**
(7–20 cm)

feather-like
branches

distinct
main
branch

Plumaria
(5–10 cm)
dingy hanging
tufts

There are very many fine, red seaweeds; those illustrated are some of the most common ones

GREEN SEAWEEDS

Codium
(up to 30 cm)
middle shore in
deep pools

Cladophora
(7–8 cm)
middle shore in
tufts on rocks

Sea Lettuce (Ulva)
(10–20 cm)
most of shore in summer

Enteromorpha
(10–30 cm)
most of shore,
particularly near
freshwater springs
spring – summer

LICHENS

Lichens are most often greyish-green
plants that grow on rocks, stones, roofs,
soil, trees, and bushes.

Collect as many different kinds as
you can.
If they are powdery, scrape a small
quantity of powder on to a glass slide
and look at it under a microscope.

If they are leafy, put a small piece on a
glass slide, look first at the upper side
and then the lower under a microscope.
Break the leafy part, called the *thallus*,
and look carefully at the broken edge.

You will see that the lichen thallus is
really made up of two plants growing
together to make one. Most of the thallus
is made up of white fungus hyphae (see page 6).
Among the hyphae numerous minute
algae grow (see page 28).

Lichens are able to grow where other plants
would die, because the algae make the
food, and the fungus provides the water by
soaking it up when it rains.

HOW TO MOUNT LICHENS

Dry them, mount them on card or in shallow boxes,
cover them with cellophane. Label them (see page 5).

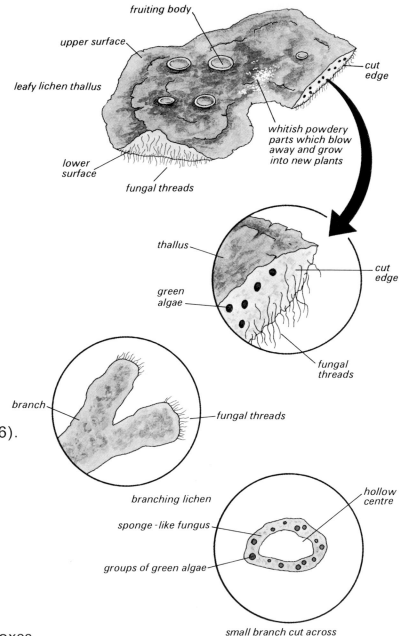

Many lichens can be used to make dyes. Boil the lichen and the cloth to be dyed together in water for several hours.
Try as many different lichens as possible to see how many different coloured dyes you can make.

CLUES TO NAMING LICHENS

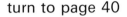

1. If the lichen thallus (see page 38) forms a greyish green, blackish, or orange crust on stone or wood, it is an ENCRUSTING LICHEN.

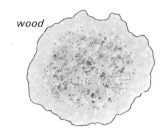

turn to page 40

2. If the lichen thallus is greyish green, blackish, or orange, flat, leaf-like, and grows over wood, stones, or soil, it is a LEAFY LICHEN.

turn to page 41

3. If the greyish-green, leaf-like thallus is rather small and covered with fruiting bodies that look like one of these, it is a CUP LICHEN (Cladonia).

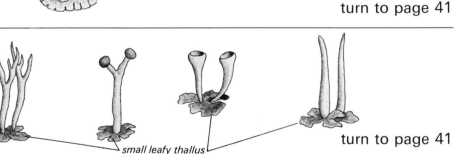

small leafy thallus

turn to page 41

4. If the greyish green thallus is branched, and most often attached by a holdfast to rocks or branches, it is a BRANCHING LICHEN.

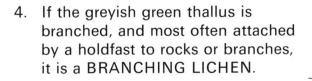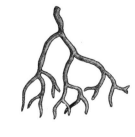

turn to page 40

ENCRUSTING LICHENS

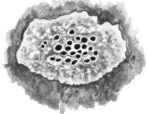

**Black Shields
(Lecanora)**
on rocks and walls

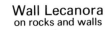

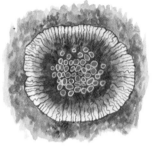

Wall Lecanora
on rocks and walls

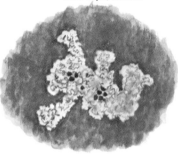

Scattered Lecanora
on limestone concrete, mortar

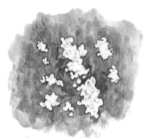

Lecidia
wall tops, bricks

often found
in towns

Scribble Lichens
on trees

BRANCHING LICHENS

Beard Lichen (Usnea)
on trees

Evernia
flattened thallus whose
upper and lower surfaces
look different
trees and fences

Ramalina
flattened thallus whose
upper and lower surfaces look alike
trees and fences

Branching Cladonia
clumps on heaths

LEAFY LICHENS

Dog-tooth Lichen (Peltigera)
on soil

Physcia
most often forms
circular clusters
on trees, walls

Parmelia
on trees,
fences, rocks

Yellow Scales Lichen (Xanthoria)
stones, roofs

CUP LICHENS (CLADONIA)

Common Cup Lichen
walls, tree stumps

Red-Topped Cladonias
heaths

Slender Cladonia
peaty heaths, peaty soil,
tree trunks

LIVERWORTS

Liverworts often grow in wet places. The leaf-like part which is very green is called a *thallus*. Small plants can be mounted in a drop of water and looked at under a lens or microscope.

Spores (see page 3) grow in fruiting bodies (capsules) that burst when ripe. Slender, spring-like elators help to scatter the spores, which grow if they fall on wet places.

If you look at a burst capsule under a microscope you will see spores and elators.

Some liverworts produce both spores and tiny bud-like parts called 'gemmae'. The gemmae fall to the ground and quickly grow into new plants. Try to grow gemmae by putting a few on damp soil in a container (see page 5).

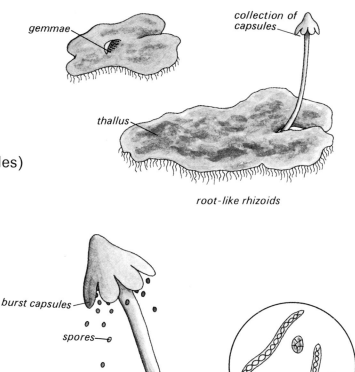

gemmae
collection of capsules
thallus
root-like rhizoids
burst capsules
spores
spore
elators with twisted bands

CLUES TO NAMING LIVERWORTS

1. If the thallus is large and leaf-like (see illustration above)

turn to page 43

2. If the thallus is very small, has flat, leaf-like parts, without midribs, and all the cells are roundish, it may be a LEAFY LIVERWORT.

   (See also Flat Fork Moss, page 49, clue 7.)

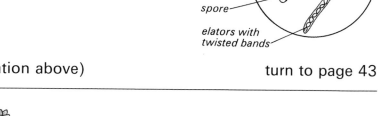

capsule
roundish cells

turn to page 43

LIVERWORTS wet places on paths, stream banks, woods

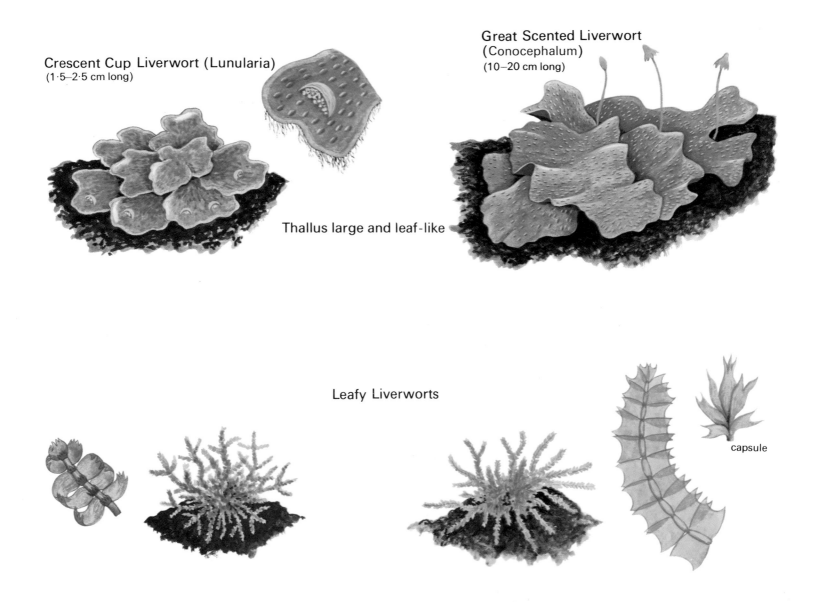

Crescent Cup Liverwort (Lunularia)
(1·5–2·5 cm long)

Great Scented Liverwort
(Conocephalum)
(10–20 cm long)

Thallus large and leaf-like

Leafy Liverworts

capsule

MOSSES

Moss plants are small. Their leaves grow close together on a slender stem. They most often grow in masses in damp shady places. The spores of mosses (see page 3) grow in fruiting bodies called *capsules*.

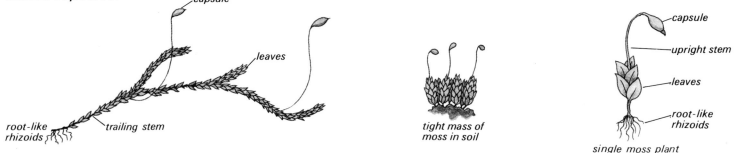

Make a collection of as many different moss plants as you can. You will sometimes find several different kinds in one clump. Mount them on card under clear self-adhesive plastic. Label them (see page 5). If the plants grow in tight clumps, use two large pins or needles to separate them before you mount them.

If you are mounting long trailing mosses, mount them so that you can see how they branch. This will help you when you are trying to name them.

trailing moss mounted and labelled

Always dry some of each kind of moss you find. When you are ready to examine it, soak it in water until it looks fresh again.

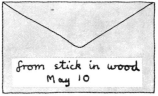

envolope with dried moss

Different kinds of mosses produce capsules at different times of the year. Collect mosses with capsules at each season of the year. Label pages of your moss book *spring, summer, autumn, winter,* and mount the mosses with capsules on the correct page.

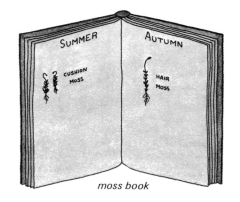

moss book

Look at a moss capsule under a microscope or lens with good magnification.

If it has a cap and lid, pull them off; on the end of the capsule you will see the teeth which open in dry weather so that the spores from inside can be shaken out by the wind, and blown to new ground where they will grow.

Try to shake or squeeze some spores out of the capsule.
Watch what happens to the teeth of a dry capsule when you put a drop of water over it.

Look at the leaves of moss plants under a microscope.
The box-like structures you can see are cells.
You can see them in moss leaves because they are arranged in a single layer, but in fact all plants and animals are made up of minute cells. The leaves of different mosses have different shaped cells.

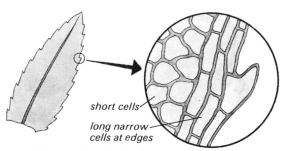

short cells

long narrow cells at edges

CLUES TO NAMING MOSSES
Examine each plant carefully (see page 44 and above).

(see also pages 46, clues 1 and 2; 47, clue 1; and 49 clues 6 and 8)

1. If the plant has long, trailing, branched stems that spread out over the surface on which it grows

turn to page 46, clues 1 and 2

2. If the plant grows upright and is most often unbranched

tree-like branching at top

upright stem

turn to page 46, clues 3 and 4

From page 45, clue 1

1. If the plant grows in spongy masses in wet places, most often has branches arranged in pairs around the stem, and has both green and colourless cells in the leaf, it is a BOG MOSS (Sphagnum).

leaf cells

long green cells

colourless cells with strands for strengthening

turn to page 50

2. If the branches of the plant are not arranged in pairs, and most of the leaf cells are long and narrow, it may be WILLOW MOSS or one of the FEATHER MOSSES.

long, narrow cells

turn to page 48

From page 45, clue 2

3. If the plant is very small (2 cm or less), grows in dense patches, and has a hair-like point on its leaves, it may be a DWARF MOSS or SILVERY THREAD MOSS.

one leaf

hair-like point

turn to clue 1 below and clues 2–4, top of page 47

4. If all the plants grow in loose patches, and a single plant can easily be separated from the rest.

turn to clues 1–3, bottom of page 47 or page 49

From clue 3 above

1. If the plant has tightly overlapping leaves and grows in silvery patches on pavements and wall tops, it may be SILVERY THREAD MOSS.

one leaf

silvery point

midrib

capsule

tightly overlapping leaves

turn to page 51

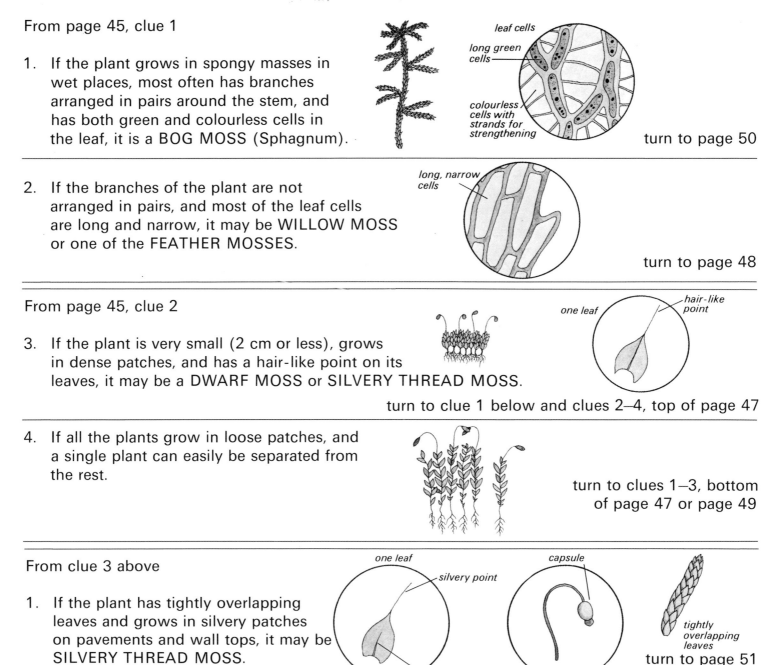

Continued from page 46, clue 3

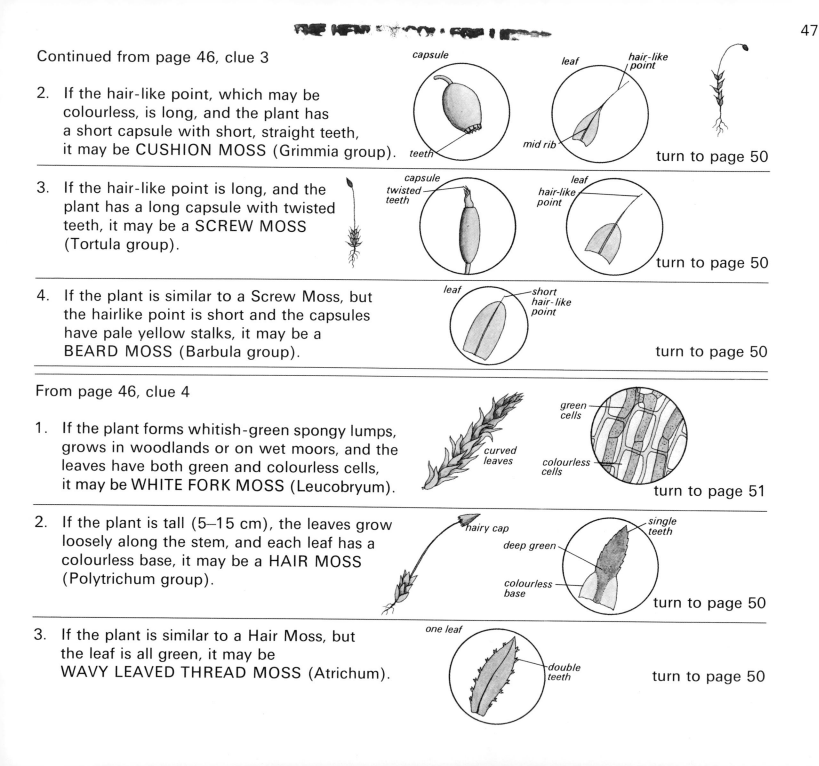

2. If the hair-like point, which may be colourless, is long, and the plant has a short capsule with short, straight teeth, it may be CUSHION MOSS (Grimmia group).

turn to page 50

3. If the hair-like point is long, and the plant has a long capsule with twisted teeth, it may be a SCREW MOSS (Tortula group).

turn to page 50

4. If the plant is similar to a Screw Moss, but the hairlike point is short and the capsules have pale yellow stalks, it may be a BEARD MOSS (Barbula group).

turn to page 50

From page 46, clue 4

1. If the plant forms whitish-green spongy lumps, grows in woodlands or on wet moors, and the leaves have both green and colourless cells, it may be WHITE FORK MOSS (Leucobryum).

turn to page 51

2. If the plant is tall (5–15 cm), the leaves grow loosely along the stem, and each leaf has a colourless base, it may be a HAIR MOSS (Polytrichum group).

turn to page 50

3. If the plant is similar to a Hair Moss, but the leaf is all green, it may be WAVY LEAVED THREAD MOSS (Atrichum).

turn to page 50

MOSSES

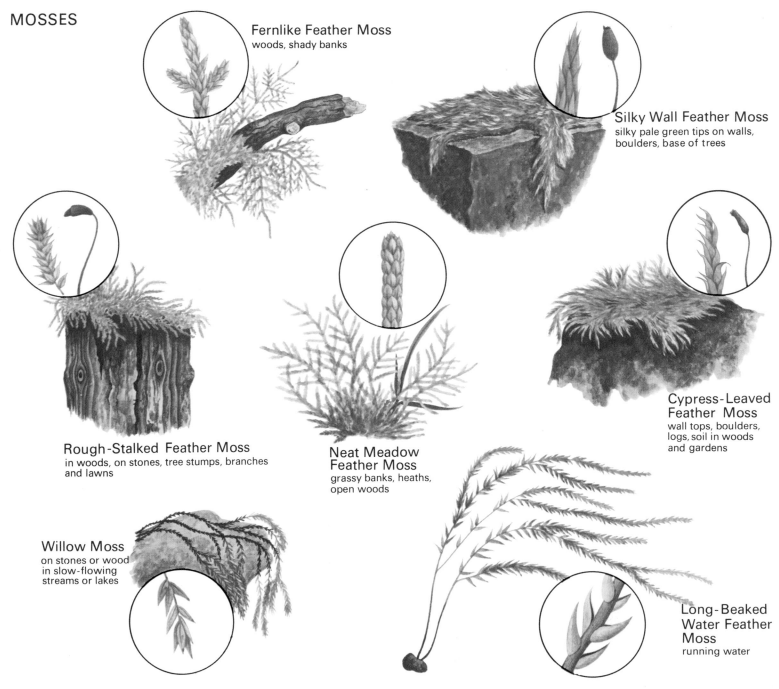

Fernlike Feather Moss
woods, shady banks

Silky Wall Feather Moss
silky pale green tips on walls,
boulders, base of trees

Rough-Stalked Feather Moss
in woods, on stones, tree stumps, branches
and lawns

**Neat Meadow
Feather Moss**
grassy banks, heaths,
open woods

**Cypress-Leaved
Feather Moss**
wall tops, boulders,
logs, soil in woods
and gardens

Willow Moss
on stones or wood
in slow-flowing
streams or lakes

**Long-Beaked
Water Feather
Moss**
running water

Continued from page 47

ball of gemmae

one gemma

4. If the plant is small (1–3 cm) and the part that looks like a fruiting body is a stalk with a yellowish-green ball of bud-like gemmae (see page 42) on the end it is a BUD-HEADED THREAD MOSS.

turn to page 51

5. If the leaves are very long, pointed, and curved to one side, it may be a FORK MOSS (Dicranum group).

turn to page 51

6. If the upper leaves form a rosette, the capsule is bent, and the cells of the leaf are almost rectangular, it may be a CORD MOSS (Funaria).

bent capsule

leaf cells

rosette of leaves

turn to page 50

7. If the leaves are flattened, arranged in two rows along the stem, and have a small 'pocket' near the base of each leaf, it may be a FLAT FORK MOSS (Fissidens group) (see also Leafy Liverworts, page 42).

one leaf

midrib

'pocket'

turn to page 51

8. If the plant is not like any of these, has leaf cells which are more-or-less square, except round the edges, where they are long, and a capsule which droops, it may be a THREAD MOSS (Byrum and Mnium groups).

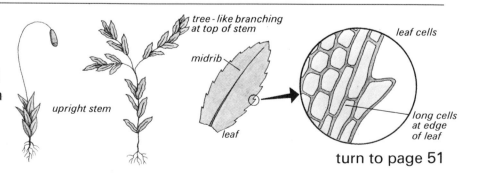

tree-like branching at top of stem

midrib

leaf cells

upright stem

leaf

long cells at edge of leaf

turn to page 51

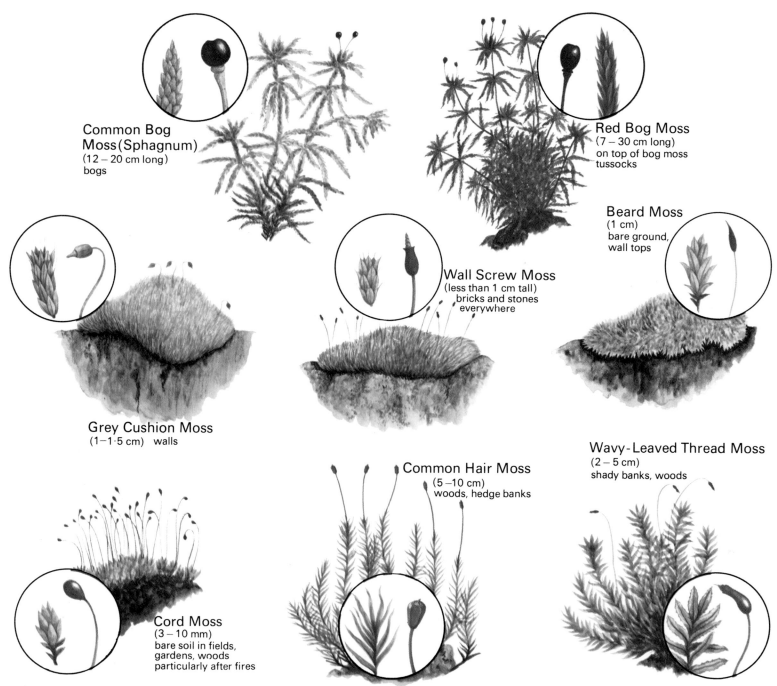

**Common Bog
Moss(Sphagnum)**
(12 – 20 cm long)
bogs

Red Bog Moss
(7 – 30 cm long)
on top of bog moss
tussocks

Beard Moss
(1 cm)
bare ground,
wall tops

Wall Screw Moss
(less than 1 cm tall)
bricks and stones
everywhere

Grey Cushion Moss
(1 – 1·5 cm) walls

Wavy-Leaved Thread Moss
(2 – 5 cm)
shady banks, woods

Common Hair Moss
(5 – 10 cm)
woods, hedge banks

Cord Moss
(3 – 10 mm)
bare soil in fields,
gardens, woods
particularly after fires

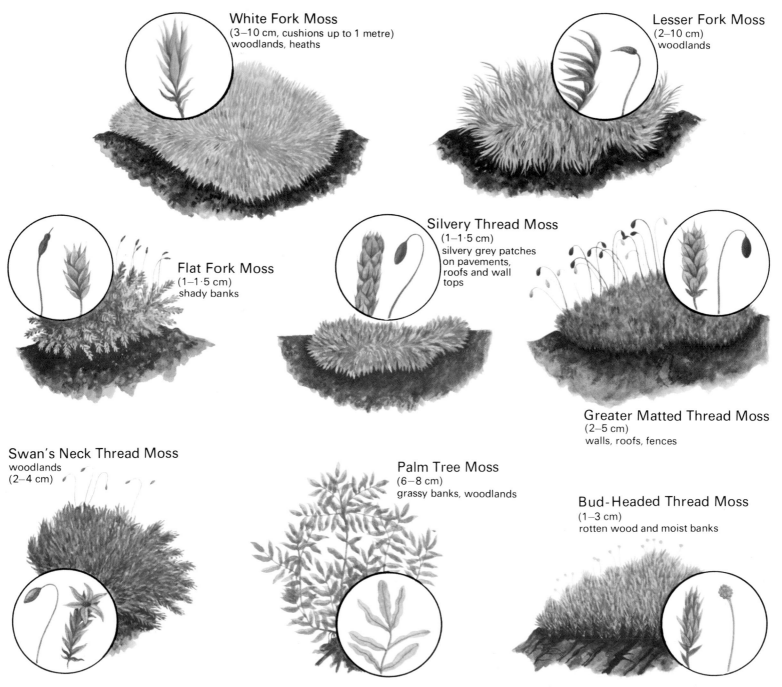

White Fork Moss
(3–10 cm, cushions up to 1 metre)
woodlands, heaths

Lesser Fork Moss
(2–10 cm)
woodlands

Flat Fork Moss
(1–1·5 cm)
shady banks

Silvery Thread Moss
(1–1·5 cm)
silvery grey patches
on pavements,
roofs and wall
tops

Greater Matted Thread Moss
(2–5 cm)
walls, roofs, fences

Swan's Neck Thread Moss
woodlands
(2–4 cm)

Palm Tree Moss
(6–8 cm)
grassy banks, woodlands

Bud-Headed Thread Moss
(1–3 cm)
rotten wood and moist banks

FERNS

Ferns are green plants with large leaves called *fronds*. The fronds are deeply divided into leaflets called *pinnae*. A pinna may be divided again into *pinnules*.

The young fronds grow coiled up at the end of the short underground stem.

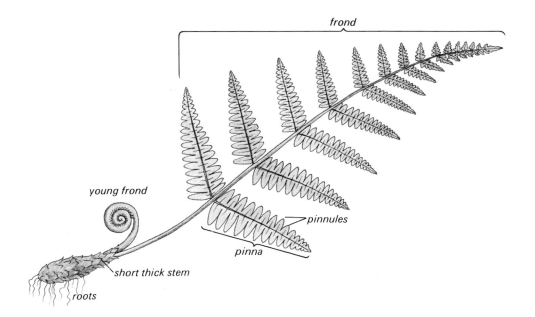

It is illegal to dig up wild ferns, but you may collect a frond from each plant. You can buy fern plants from nursery gardens.

Collect as many different kinds as you can (see page 5).

If you are mounting a collection of ferns, turn some of the pinnules over to show the clusters of spore cases (see page 53).

During the summer and autumn the spore cases grow in clusters on the underside of the fronds. They may be protected by a cover (see page 53).

In order to name your ferns you will need to look closely at the arrangement and shape of the clusters of spore cases. Use a magnifying lens or microscope.

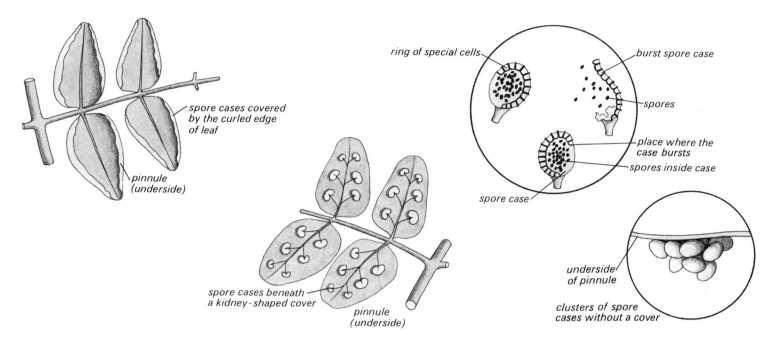

spore cases covered by the curled edge of leaf

pinnule (underside)

ring of special cells

burst spore case

spores

place where the case bursts

spores inside case

spore case

spore cases beneath a kidney-shaped cover

pinnule (underside)

underside of pinnule

clusters of spore cases without a cover

HOW TO GROW FERNS

It is possible to grow ferns from spores (see page 5) that you collect from both wild and cultivated plants, but it may be several months before small fern plants can be seen.

You will need a clear plastic box or glass butter dish with a lid, half full of damp soil or peat.

Shake the ripe spores onto the soil, put the lid on and leave in a light place.

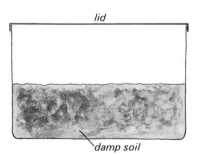

lid

damp soil

In Spring you may find tiny plants growing in soil around bigger fern plants.

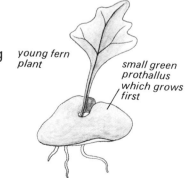

young fern plant

small green prothallus which grows first

CLUES TO NAMING FERNS

1. If the spore cases
   grow on special fronds
   that look like this,
   it is ROYAL FERN
   (Osmunda).

part of frond with spore cases

part of leafy frond

pinnules

turn to page 58

2. If the spore cases
   grow on special fronds
   in the centre of the
   plant, and the fronds
   look like this, it
   is HARD FERN
   (Blechnum).

frond with spore cases

leafy frond

turn to page 58

3. If all the fronds look alike

see below and pages 55, 56 and 57

From clue 3 above.

1. If the frond is single, it is
   either HART'S TONGUE FERN
   (Phillitis)
   or BIRD'S NEST SPLEENWORT.

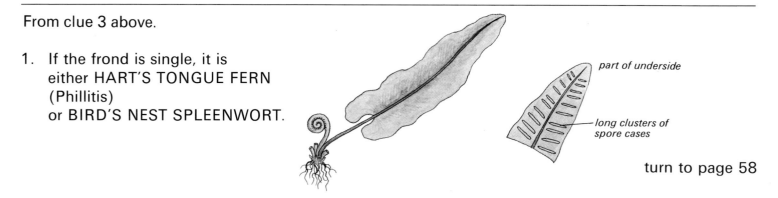

part of underside

long clusters of spore cases

turn to page 58

From page 54

2. If the fronds have slender wiry black stems it is MAIDENHAIR FERN.

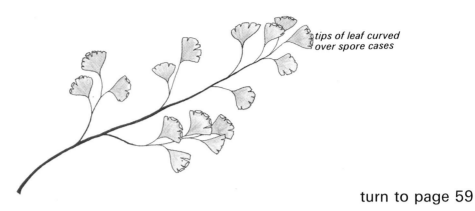

tips of leaf curved over spore cases

turn to page 59

3. If the fronds look like this, and the spore cases grow along the edges, which are curved over them, it may be RIBBON FERN (Pteris).

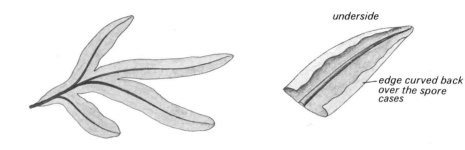

underside

edge curved back over the spore cases

turn to page 58

4. If the fronds grow up to 200 cms tall, and have pinnae widely apart on strong, shining leaf stalks, it is BRACKEN.

turn to page 59

Continued from page 55

5. If the fronds and clusters of spores look like one of these, go to the pages shown.

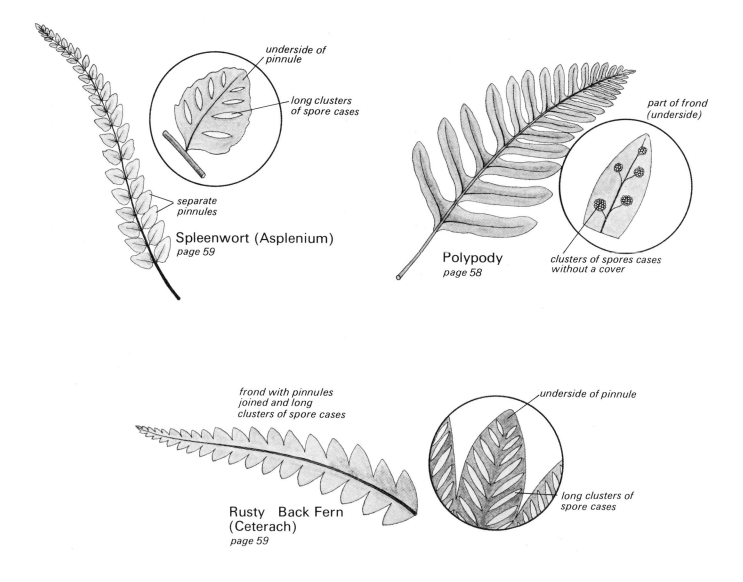

underside of pinnule

long clusters of spore cases

separate pinnules

Spleenwort (Asplenium)
page 59

part of frond (underside)

Polypody
page 58

clusters of spores cases without a cover

frond with pinnules joined and long clusters of spore cases

underside of pinnule

Rusty Back Fern (Ceterach)
page 59

long clusters of spore cases

6. If the pinnae of the fronds grow close together on the leaf stalk and the covers of the spore cases are shaped like one of these, go to the page shown.

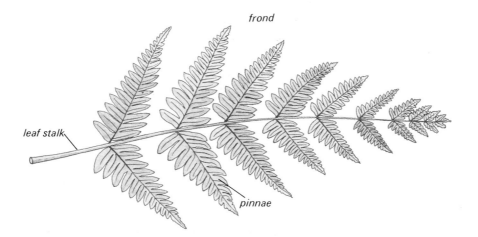

frond

leaf stalk

pinnae

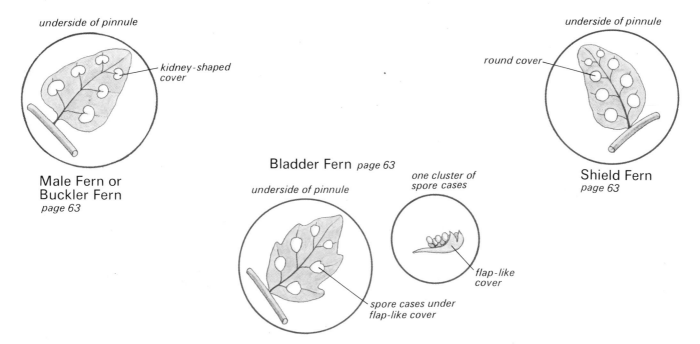

underside of pinnule

kidney-shaped cover

Male Fern or Buckler Fern
page 63

Bladder Fern *page 63*

underside of pinnule

one cluster of spore cases

flap-like cover

spore cases under flap-like cover

underside of pinnule

round cover

Shield Fern
page 63

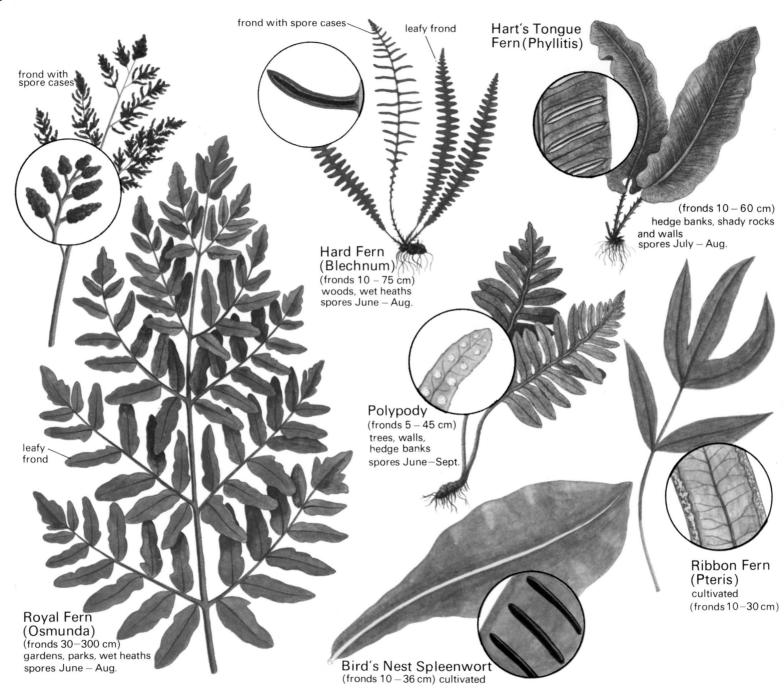

frond with
spore cases

frond with spore cases

leafy frond

Hart's Tongue
Fern (Phyllitis)

(fronds 10 – 60 cm)
hedge banks, shady rocks
and walls
spores July – Aug.

Hard Fern
(Blechnum)
(fronds 10 – 75 cm)
woods, wet heaths
spores June – Aug.

Polypody
(fronds 5 – 45 cm)
trees, walls,
hedge banks
spores June – Sept.

Ribbon Fern
(Pteris)
cultivated
(fronds 10 – 30 cm)

leafy
frond

Royal Fern
(Osmunda)
(fronds 30 – 300 cm)
gardens, parks, wet heaths
spores June – Aug.

Bird's Nest Spleenwort
(fronds 10 – 36 cm) cultivated

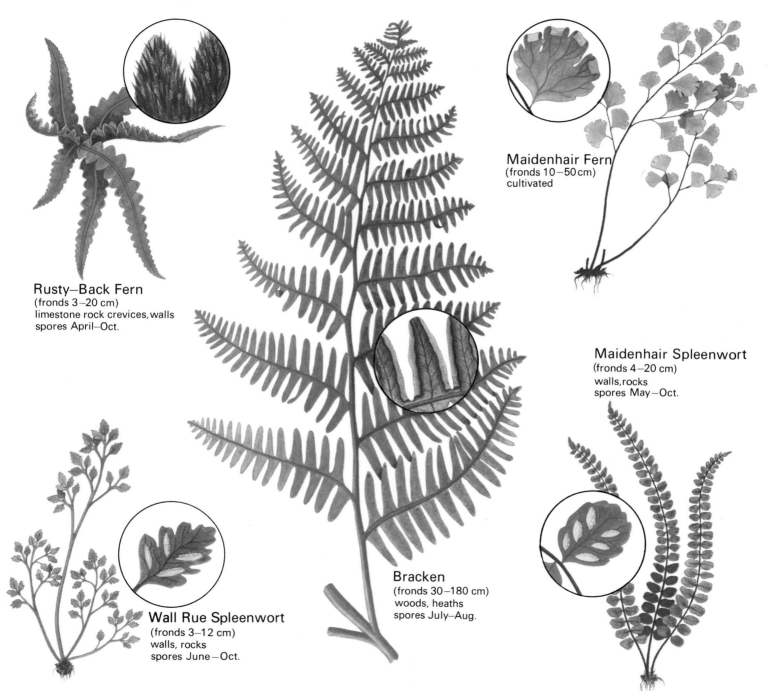

Rusty—Back Fern
(fronds 3—20 cm)
limestone rock crevices, walls
spores April—Oct.

Maidenhair Fern
(fronds 10—50 cm)
cultivated

Maidenhair Spleenwort
(fronds 4—20 cm)
walls, rocks
spores May—Oct.

Wall Rue Spleenwort
(fronds 3—12 cm)
walls, rocks
spores June—Oct.

Bracken
(fronds 30—180 cm)
woods, heaths
spores July—Aug.

HORSETAILS

In early spring the jointed, green stems of Horsetails begin to grow from creeping underground stems. They have whorls of branches.

The leaves form tiny, brown sheaths around the stems at the joints.

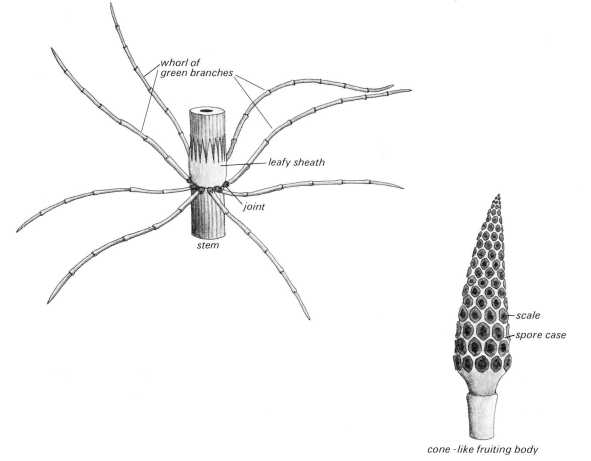

whorl of green branches

leafy sheath

joint

stem

scale

spore case

cone-like fruiting body

The cone-like fruiting bodies, in which the spores grow, die quickly.

If you look at a fruiting body under a magnifying lens, you will see rows of spore cases.

If you shake some spores onto a glass slide and look at them under a microscope, you will see the spring-like threads, called *elators* on them. These help to project the spores into the air. Those that land on suitable ground grow.

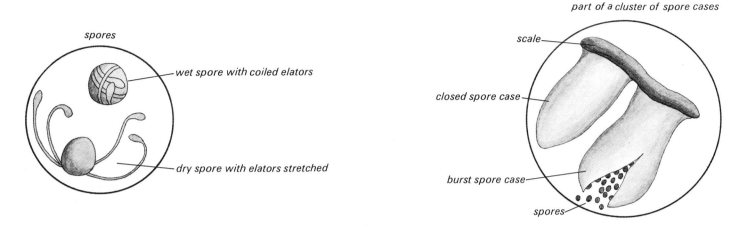

spores

wet spore with coiled elators

dry spore with elators stretched

part of a cluster of spore cases

scale

closed spore case

burst spore case

spores

HOW TO GROW HORSETAILS

If you want to see how Horsetails start to grow, scatter some spores on a piece of sterile clay pot or brick, or damp blotting paper, placed in a container that has a lid.

(To sterilize, boil the piece of clay pot or brick for ten minutes: leave to cool.)

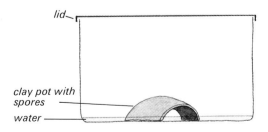

lid

clay pot with spores

water

the first plant (prothallus) 3 - 4 weeks old

The Horsetail plant will grow from this.
turn to page 62.

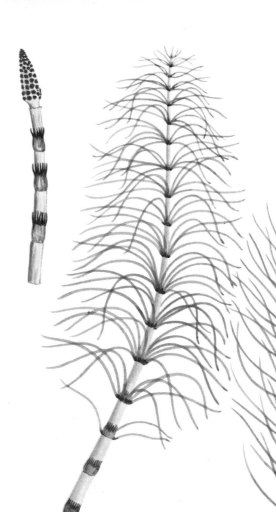

cones on top
of branched stems

Greater Horsetail
(90 – 180 cm tall, separate
cone stems 20 – 40 cm)
wet, shady banks
spores April

Common Horsetail
(20 – 80 cm tall, separate
cone stems 10 – 25 cm)
wet meadows, hedge banks
spores April

Water Horsetail
(50 – 140 cm tall)
edges of lakes,
ponds, ditches
spores June, July

Marsh Horsetail
(10 – 60 cm tall)
marshes, wet woods
and meadows
spores May – July

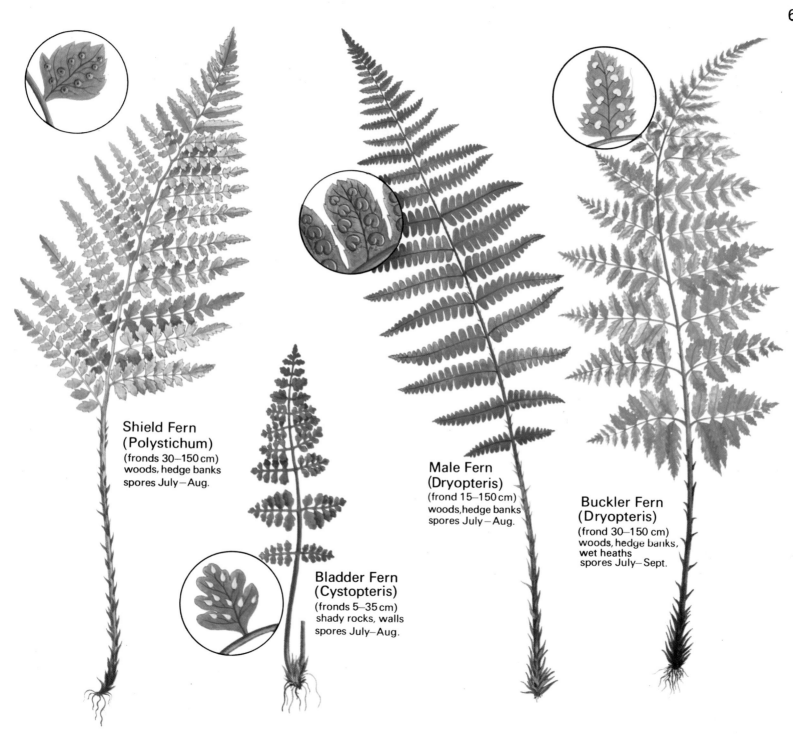

**Shield Fern
(Polystichum)**
(fronds 30—150 cm)
woods, hedge banks
spores July—Aug.

**Bladder Fern
(Cystopteris)**
(fronds 5—35 cm)
shady rocks, walls
spores July—Aug.

**Male Fern
(Dryopteris)**
(frond 15—150 cm)
woods, hedge banks
spores July—Aug.

**Buckler Fern
(Dryopteris)**
(frond 30—150 cm)
woods, hedge banks,
wet heaths
spores July—Sept.

Bibliography

Allen G. and Denslow J., *Seashore Animals*. (O.U.P.)
Alvin K. L. and Kershaw K. A., *Observers' Book of Lichens*. (Warne)
Brightman F. H. and Nicholson B. E., *Oxford Book of Flowerless Plants*. (O.U.P.)
Findlay W. P. K., *Wayside and Woodland Fungi*. (Warne)
Haworth F. M., *Toadstools and Lichens*. (U.L.P.)
Hvass E. & H., *Mushrooms and Toadstools in colour*. (Blandford)
Jewell Arthur, *Observers' Book of Mosses and Liverworts*. (Warne)
Lange M. & Hora F. B., *A Guide to Mushrooms and Toadstools*. (Collins)
North Pamela, *Poisonous Plants and Fungi in colour*. (Blandford)
Rose Francis, *Observers' Book of Ferns*. (Warne)
Wakefield E. M., *Observers' Book of Common Fungi*. (Warne)

Index